The School Leader's Yea

This practical handbook offers a month-by-month guide to the curriculum, assessment, progress, and leadership over the school year. It provides a clear, comprehensive, and coherent structure to the academic year helping school leaders to prioritise their time and workload, supporting them and their team to work as efficiently and effectively as possible.

Considering the statutory and key leadership activities from admissions, induction, transitions, and parents' evenings to coursework, timetabling, assessment, staff performance, and much more, the book provides a clear plan of action to ensure school leaders have prepared their work at the optimal time over the year. Each chapter features tried-and-tested strategies to help schools put robust systems and processes in place alongside guidance on sustaining pace, developing resilience, and exam preparation and technique.

Full of practical tips to help improve progress and including real-world examples of leadership in action from leaders working in primary and secondary schools, this is essential reading for all school leaders that want their students to be as successful as they can possibly be in every lesson, every day.

Michael Harpham is the Director of School Leader Development Ltd, a leadership coach, trainer, and former headteacher. He is also the author of *Progress Plain and Simple: What Every Teacher Needs to Know About Improving Pupil Progress*.

The School Leader's Year

Month-by-Month Progress, Every Lesson, Every Day

Michael Harpham

Routledge
Taylor & Francis Group

LONDON AND NEW YORK

First published 2022
by Routledge
2 Park Square, Milton Park, Abingdon, Oxon OX14 4RN

and by Routledge
605 Third Avenue, New York, NY 10158

Routledge is an imprint of the Taylor & Francis Group, an informa business

British Library Cataloguing-in-Publication Data
A catalogue record for this book is available from the British Library

Library of Congress Cataloging-in-Publication Data
A catalog record has been requested for this book

ISBN: 978-0-367-65492-4 (hbk)
ISBN: 978-0-367-65493-1 (pbk)
ISBN: 978-1-003-12969-1 (ebk)

DOI: 10.4324/9781003129691

Typeset in Melior
by Deanta Global Publishing Services, Chennai, India

Dedicated to all the school leaders with whom I have had the privilege and pleasure to work.

And to the memory of Agnes Harpham and Rollo,
two curmudgeons who are missed more than anything in the world.

Contents

Acknowledgements

This book draws on my experience of education over 25 years, as a teacher, school leader, headteacher, researcher, and leadership coach. From the many talented and inspirational school leaders I have met along the way, I have learnt so much. Their actions and their words are all represented and encapsulated in this book.

As it is often said, life is a journey, not a destination, enriched and occasionally influenced by our fellow travellers. The creation of this book is no exception. Specific thanks must go to:

Haydon Luke, Marion Parsons, Diana Osagie, Paul Ramsey, and Susan Service for their inspiration and encouragement on my own school leadership journey.

Dr Steve Tibble for encouraging me to continue the author's journey and to blow on the spark of an idea and see what happens. Here it is.

Debbie Brown, Caroline Davies, Carl Fisher, Jane Hart, Aykut Kekilli, Jon Meier, Phil Naylor, Joe Omar, Teddy Prout, David Ritchie, Matt Smart, Clare and Dan Smith, Claire Waites, and Jessica Ward; with their invaluable insights and input, this book has become clearer and richer as a result.

Caroline Davies for the graceful illustration.

Annamarie Kino-Wylam and Molly Selby at Routledge for their continued expertise in guiding me through the whole process a second time.

Finally, to Julian, for his continued love, patience, and steadfast support.

Heartfelt thanks to all.

About the author

 With 25 years of teaching experience, 15 of those at senior leadership level, including headship, in a broad range of schools in London and the Home Counties, Michael has extensive educational and leadership experience to share.

In addition, with two master's degrees and a doctorate in educational leadership, he also brings significant authority and ability to his work.

His passion is for education. He is an educational consultant, international trainer, author, and university lecturer. He also enjoys supporting and developing staff and teams to reach their potential and, as such, is a highly experienced mentor and coach.

Michael grew up in Yorkshire and went on to study singing, piano, and composition at the Royal Academy of Music in London. When not working, he continues to enjoy the artistic side of life, especially photography (published by *The Sunday Times*) and music (performing his own work at the Royal Albert Hall).

Other hobbies include hiking up mountains (he successfully climbed Kilimanjaro for a school charity) and travelling (blogged across India and spent a year on a Fulbright Exchange with the British Council teaching Music in California).

The School Leader's Year is his second book.

Introduction

Welcome

Over my career, one of the things I am most passionate about and which continues to really motivate me is helping people be better at what they do, as individuals or as teams. Having worked with some amazing school leaders and having been part of some wonderfully effective leadership teams, through this book I want as many school leaders as possible to be just as amazing; to be as effective as they can be.

Why this book is needed

Leading schools today is more complex and more challenging than ever before, whether in dealing with the constant flurry of government directives from the Department of Education (Gillard 2018) or responding to regularly revised inspection frameworks (Ofsted 2019b), not to mention managing the occasional pandemic (DfE 2020a).

In addition, senior leaders in schools are working approximately 57 hours a week (Ofsted 2019c; DfE 2019c). Headteachers are reported to work approximately 62 hours a week, with 43% of them indicating that their workload is unmanageable, representing an increase of 36% since 2013 (Jerrim and Sims 2019). Further, these figures are significantly higher than the 1265 hours (32.4 hours per week) expected, as laid out in the School Teachers' Pay and Conditions (DfE 2019b; Ofsted 2019c).

With such pressure on school leaders to do what needs to be done, delivering the best results for the pupils, and managing the daily life of the school in such challenging and complex circumstances (Dunford 2016; Harpham 2020), there has never been a more appropriate time than the present to produce such a book. Offering a fresh contribution to the school improvement discourse, this book supports school leaders to manage and prioritise their workload and effectively maintain their course of action through ever-present turbulence. It enables them to drive progress and deliver higher-quality teaching, learning, and leadership more effectively at the best time, benefiting not only the wellbeing, but also the success of their pupils, their school community, and to society as a whole.

> **Whether from government or inspectors,**
> **never in the field of education has so much**
> **been demanded of so many,**
> **by so few.**

Further, we need school leaders to continue to add their weight to the school improvement cause:

- In 2021, of the 25,414 UK schools nationally, 4,145 (16%) were judged by the government's inspectorate, Ofsted, as "Outstanding" (DfE 2021), indicating 84% of schools were judged as not being outstanding.

■ The number of "Good" and "Outstanding" schools has fallen in the last three years from 18,823 (87% of schools) in 2017, to 18,518 (85%) in 2019 (Ofsted 2019d).

■ According to the government's end-of-key-stage measure, Progress 8, of the 6,431 secondary schools in England in 2019, 2,127 (33%) were viewed to have a negative Progress 8 score (pupils not making expected progress). Moreover, this figure has increased by 2% each year for the last three years (DfE 2021).

What that improvement might look like is the focus of this book. It seeks to coherently connect the curriculum, leadership, assessment, and the leader's school year together and provide clarification and a suggested rationale as to what school leaders do and when.

Aims and purpose of this book

A school leader's life is not lived in isolation, but in the visceral real-life world of the school, of pupils, staff, parents, Governors, neighbours, and other schools. To this end, it is important to understand that schools have to work within a set of fixed parameters. This includes the fixed number of staff (staffing) with set roles and responsibilities (job descriptions and workload), who need to deliver a prescribed curriculum (the national curriculum, DfE 2014b), through a set weekly or fortnightly timetable (fixed annual timetable), over a certain time frame (365 days a year, or 190 working days, DfE 2019b), in a set space (the school), with fixed resources (annual budget) to a set number of pupils (Pupil Admission Number) who need to demonstrate they have sufficiently learnt the curriculum (grade descriptors) and achieve a prescribed grade in set standardised national tests by a specific date (results). Thus, the work of the school leader is in successfully managing the moveable with the immoveable and the myriad of resultant tensions and problems that occur in achieving that.

In addition, if I were to ask you, how much time *should you* spend in your working day completing work that fulfils your job description that you *expect to do*, I am guessing your answer would probably be 100%. However, if I turned that question around and asked, as a leader, how much time *do you* spend in your working day on things you *didn't expect to do* (sorting a pupil incident, fixing the printer, managing an emergency staff absence, returning a parent call), what would you say? 10%? 20%? More? What we want to do with our time and what we actually do with our time sometimes (possibly often) do not match up. Hence, it is vital that we, as leaders, manage our time, our workload, and our wellbeing as effectively as possible.

WORKLOAD / TIME PRESSURE TABLE

AUTUMN TERM

Month	September	October	November	December	Total
Days in school	20	17	21	14	72 / 190
Proportion of year	11%	9%	11%	7%	38%
Workload over year (no. of activities)	28	13	9	8	58 / 146
Proportion of workload	19%	9%	6%	5%	39%
Difference	+8%	0%	-5%	-2%	+1
Pressure of Workload v Time	Very High	Low	Very Low	Low	

SPRING TERM

Month	January	February	March	April	Total
Days in school	20	15	23	12	70 / 190
Proportion of year	11%	8%	12%	6%	37%
Workload over year (no. of activities)	8	6	11	9	34 / 146
Proportion of workload	5%	4%	8%	6%	23%
Difference	-6%	-4%	-4%	0%	-14
Pressure of Workload v Time	Very Low	Low	Low	Low	

SUMMER TERM

Month	May	June	July	August	Total
Days in school	14	22	12	0	48 / 190
Proportion of year	7%	12%	6%	0%	25%
Workload over year (no. of activities)	8	22	20	4	54 / 146
Proportion of workload	5%	16%	14%	3%	38%
Difference	-2%	+4%	+8%	+3%	+13
Pressure of Workload v Time	Low	High	Very High	High	

The table above summarises the key school activities over the year covered in this book, giving us a very rough indication of the quantity of the work, by month, that school leaders need do over the year. As a result, it also gives an indication of when there are high-pressure and low-pressure points over the year.

As can be seen, high-pressure points for the school leader are mainly at the close (June and July) and opening (August and September) of the school year.

Lower pressure points are during the rest of the year, October through to May, where more energy can be expended on driving forward the work of the school and ensuring important milestones are reached. By knowing this, if we assume that 10% (minimum) of our working day is going to be taken up by things other than what is required of us, that time has to be factored into our working day, we need to be ready and able to delegate to others, or to take the phone off the hook, close the emails, and prioritise the important and the urgent, especially at those high-pressure points in the year in September, June, and July. Similarly, making time to contact pupils, staff, or parents (with good news or less good news) helps keep our time more under our control.

Schedule in time every day to deal with the known.
Schedule in time every day to deal with the unknown.

The aim of this book is to ultimately improve pupil progress by offering school leaders a structure to their work over the school year that helps them effectively organise and prioritise their work and time in a clear, comprehensive, and coherent way. The aim, to use a metaphor, is for the school leader to be like a swan, gliding, leading, seemingly effortlessly, through the school year, effectively managing each and every challenge. As a result of more effective leadership, teachers and pupils are able to work in a more effective and more successful way than would otherwise be the case, leading to greater pupil progress and success.

So, first and foremost, this book is a school leader's diary that tells you what you need to be doing and when over the school year. From September and the arrival of the first pupil, through to August, when the school doors close, and that last pupil leaves having received their (fantastic) results.

This book is also a how-to-do-it handbook that shows you how to do something that is high-quality, tried-and-tested, and works. It helps. When needed, first-rate examples are provided, sign-posted and accessible (all year!) to help model what you need to do.

Thus, this book, aimed at both primary and secondary school leaders, offers the "when" and "why" of education, giving a clear, structured, and coherent plan of action to the year for schools (Hall 2020). As the year progresses, curriculum needs change, from embedding systems and processes and getting into good habits at the start of the year, through sustaining pace and developing resilience in the middle of the year, to finessing exam preparation and technique at the end of the year. The book, then, helps school leaders check they have sufficiently prepared their important work at the optimal time over the school year.

Features of the book and how it can be used

Taking over 30 key activities for which leaders are responsible in a school, I have suggested months when they can be prepared, actioned, and reviewed. Some activities only occur once a year (e.g. appeals) and so are prepared for, actioned, and reviewed only once. Other activities are recurring throughout the year (e.g. implementing the next Scheme of Work) and so are repeated deliberately, to help support the reader by having everything needed to read for that month in one place, thus saving the leader/reader time and effort. This creates over 100 key actions over the year for school leaders. Unless otherwise stated, the information given is applicable to both middle and senior leaders, in both primary and secondary phases.

KEY SCHOOL LEADERSHIP ACTIVITIES THROUGH THE YEAR (A–Z)				
Appeals	Assemblies	Assessment	Budget	Capital bids
Census	Coursework/ Revision	End/start of term	Exams and careers	School Development Plan (SDP)/SEF/continuing professional development (CPD)
Induction	Integrated Framework	Documentation	Monitoring/ tracking	Options
Parents' Evenings	Policies	Admissions and pupil recruitment	Quality assurance	Repairs/maintenance
Routines and duties	Schemes of Work	Staff performance	Staff recruitment	Statutory duties
Surveys	Tests	Timetable	Transition	Website and display

The rationale for this is that for each key school activity, (a) it is important to reflect, identify the positives, and learn the lessons from previous work, as this might have a bearing on current action; (b) current action needs instigating and possibly completing in the present before (c) the preparation of future work. At the start of each month there is a list, so you can see in advance what lies ahead. This is followed by a rationale as to why activities can be completed in that order, with more detailed descriptions of each of the actions needed. Drawing on Atul Gawande's excellent *Checklist Manifesto: How to Get Things Right* (2011), there is a checklist at the end of the month to ensure everything that needs to be done has been done.

Each term and each month's actions are categorised using the following key:

SYMBOL	MEANING
⟳	Action that **prepares** for the activity in the future
⟫	Action that **supports** the activity currently being done
👍	Action that **analyses, evaluates, and celebrates** the activity after completion
Activity	**Higher priority** (Statutory activity/statutory related activity)
Activity	**Lower priority** (Non-statutory activity)

In addition, to illustrate and offer some real-world examples of leadership in action, once or twice each month there are some key lessons in leadership, or "moments that count". These are either written by me (or other school staff) working in primary and secondary schools and provide some real-life wisdom in the form of short vignettes.

Summary

This book is not an exact science. What is offered here for school leaders is a framework, a structure to help prioritise your work. If the suggested order or timing is different for you, change the order or timing. If the suggested order or timing acts as a catalyst and supports you to lead as effectively as you can, so much the better.

We all strive for perfection. We all get things right and occasionally we forget to do things. We are human. It is likely that we know what we need to do today, the next few days, possibly even this week. It is less likely that we know what we need to do over the next few weeks, this month, or this year.

This book is therefore offered as a key for you, to help you know what you need to do and when, to help you lead more successfully and as a result, for you and your team, to be a little closer to perfection.

Welcome to the school leader's year!

Autumn term: Sowing seeds

DOI: 10.4324/9781003129691-1

AUTUMN TERM SUMMARY			
KEY	**STATUTORY ACTIVITY (HIGHER PRIORITY)**		**NON-STATUTORY ACTIVITY (LOWER PRIORITY)**
👍 Action that evaluates and celebrates previous work	»» Action that supports current work		◷ Action that prepares future work
A–Z of key school activities	September	October	November	December
Admissions	◷	»»		
Appeals	◷ »» 👍			
Assemblies	»»			
Assessment programme	»»			
Budget	»»			
Capital bids			◷	»»
Census	◷	»»		
Coursework, Catch Up, and Revision programmes	◷	»»	»»	»»
End/start of term	👍		◷	»»
Exams and careers	👍			
Improvement Plans/ School Evaluation Form(SEF)/continuing professional development (CPD)	👍 ◷ »»	»»		»»
Induction and Summer School	»» 👍			
Integrated framework	👍	◷		»»
Monitoring and tracking		»»		
Options			◷	
Parents' Evenings		◷		
Performance appraisal and pay	◷	»»		
Policies	»»			
Pupil recruitment/destinations	👍	◷	»»	
Quality assurance	◷	»»		
Repairs and maintenance	👍			
Routines and duties	»» 👍			
Schemes of Work/Personal, Social, Health, and Economic education (PSHE)		»»		»»
Staff recruitment			»»	
Statutory requirements	»»			
Surveys		◷	»»	👍
Tests			◷ »»	👍
Timetable	»» 👍			
Website, displays, and Open Evening	»»	👍		

September

September is the start of a new academic year. A time where lessons from the previous year can be learnt and the course of action for the new year set.

September needs to be experienced with clarity.

DOI: 10.4324/9781003129691-2

Introduction: September

So here we are. Day 1, Week 1. Everything is fresh and new and has the air of optimism as time and space stretch into the distance. The following strategies are for school leaders to use at either the whole school or the department level. Here is what you have ahead of you in September.

SEPTEMBER SUMMARY		
KEY		
👍 **Action that evaluates and celebrates previous work**	》》 **Action that supports current work**	🕒 **Action that prepares future work**
Statutory activity (higher priority)		**Non-statutory activity (lower priority)**
Action	*Leaders*	*School focus for September*
👍	All leaders	Evaluate annual exam results
👍	Senior leaders	Evaluate pupil recruitment and destinations
👍	Senior leaders	Evaluate the repairs and maintenance programme
👍	All leaders	Evaluate the integrated work of the school
》》	All leaders	All statutory requirements are in place and live
》》	Senior leaders	Staff/pupil induction successfully completed
》》	All leaders	School Timetable/duties/routines/website in place
》》	All leaders	All policies go live and are implemented
🕒 》》	All leaders	Arrange and send off Exam Appeals
》》	Senior leaders	Implement Assemblies/Inspiring People programme
》》	All leaders	Assessment programme in place
👍🕒》》	All leaders	Update School/Faculty Improvement/continuing professional development (CPD) Plans
🕒	All leaders	Agree internal and external quality assurance
》》	Senior leaders	Finalise and implement a revised budget plan
》》	All leaders	Carry out successful Open Evening and Open Week

SEPTEMBER SUMMARY		
KEY		
👍 **Action that evaluates and celebrates previous work**	》》 **Action that supports current work**	⏱ **Action that prepares future work**
Statutory activity (higher priority)		**Non-statutory activity (lower priority)**
⏱	All leaders	Prepare performance appraisal process/pay documentation
⏱	Senior leaders	Prepare Admissions arrangements
⏱	All leaders	Prepare Coursework, Catch Up, and Revision programmes
⏱	All leaders	Prepare for census
👍	All leaders	Evaluate timetabling, appeals, induction, and start of year
👍	All leaders	Evaluate duties and routines

As September starts, prepare key messages for staff, students, governors, and parents so that as a school community, you set the tone for a positive and constructive year ahead. In your regular team meetings, create an opportunity to discuss the following standing agenda items:

- **Staffing and safeguarding**: Are there any staffing and/or safeguarding concerns to be urgently addressed this month?

- **Calendar**: Are there any pinch points this month which need to be carefully managed beforehand?

- **Trips and school activities**: Are there any trips or large group activities this month, or during the October half term, which need to be carefully managed?

- **Website and communications**: Is the website up to date and are parents/pupils/staff clear about what is happening this month? Is there robust, challenging, and engaging online work available for pupils to complete if needed?

- **Inspection ready**: Which areas need addressing this month to ensure we are on track with our work?

The rationale for the other actions taking place this month, and in this order, include that an action is *more important* or needs doing *more urgently*, has a higher priority and therefore comes earlier in the month and vice versa. An action may be *part of a process* and so must happen before one action, but after another. Also, certain actions are *fixed* to events outside of the school's control and so these actions are tied to a particular date in the calendar (for example, external exams), or are actions *related to a fixed* event. Thus, an analysis and evaluation of the annual exam results and the subsequent destinations of those pupils; the completion of the repairs and maintenance programme; and the effectiveness of the integrated work of the school (the curriculum, teaching, leadership, and budget), must take place at the start of September after the results have been published and the summer holidays have come to a close. This must also be followed by a celebration of each of these.

A calm, orderly return to school is the next imminent activity, with all statutory requirements and what is needed on the school's website in place, a successful induction of the pupils and staff, with duties, routines, the timetable, and school policies going live to help the school community to hit the ground running from the start. Once school is back in full swing, the communication related to examination appeals between parents, ex-pupils, and the exam boards can begin. Concurrently, the assemblies, inspiring minds, and assessments programmes commence, alongside the school, faculty, and CPD improvement plans being updated, informing the internal and external quality assurance programmes, which in turn inform the budget for the year ahead. With almost all things retrospective being complete and all things current underway, the school can start to look forwards and prepare for the urgent arrival of the Open Evening and Open Week.

In October we see the signing off of the old and setting up of the new Performance Appraisal process, which requires detailed planning in September. The end of September and early October also sees the need for admissions arrangements to be reviewed as well as the first round of marking being completed. This creates an opportunity to see how well pupils are on track with their work and provide feedback and additional support or intervention, requiring leaders to think through and plan in September how this will look. The all-important census also takes place in October for the first time. Sufficient preparation with relevant new staff and key personnel (administrative staff, pastoral leaders, and the Special Educational Needs Coordinator (SENCO) in particular) as to the data required will help deliver a smooth and efficient process.

Finally, as September comes to a close and the whirlwind that was the start of term begins to dissipate, it allows a moment of reflection and celebration as to how well the timetable, the exam appeals process, staff and pupil induction, including the Summer School, the start of the year, and settling into routines all went. The end of September is the pause for breath, the look around and check – was that the start of the year we wanted to see, and have we made a good start? The answer should be an unequivocal "Yes!"

(All leaders)   **Annual exam results**

Securing progress by knowing what leadership, teaching, and learning strategies are effective

Reporting the annual exam results is the culmination of thousands of hours of work by hundreds of people. Part of being a leader is not just about reading data but about identifying the factors leading to that data. What lies behind the data? Why is one set of data better with the same set of teachers and the same set of pupils in the same school? What is going on to create this situation? There are a number of websites that can help with analysing school results (which you usually pay for), a couple of which I have indicated in chapter 15. To save time and help write your report, here are some points to consider beforehand:

▓ RAG rate grades to provide an initial picture of the level of success of the teaching and learning in the classroom in relation to the targets set.

> **Green = Above expectation = Teaching and learning has been more effective than expected.**
>
> **Amber = At expectation = Teaching and learning has been as effective as expected.**
>
> **Red = Below expectation = Teaching and learning has not been as effective as expected.**

▓ Identify what is going well so you start your narrative from a position of strength.

▓ Identify any patterns in what needs improving (the RED data). This helps focus the narrative on issues to be resolved and informs the narrative with future actions to capitalise on a potential increase in progress.

▓ Have these RED patterns happened before? If so, prepare your defence!

> **Be aware of, and ready for, a potential trap! Any issues that have arisen under your leadership will reflect on you. Why didn't you do something about these issues before? Be ready for this.**

▓ Maintain a balanced and laser-like focus on the **cause** (successful/poor leadership/teaching) and **effect** (successful/poor learning) to help improve and increase progress.

■ When progress is less than sufficient, check how clear, coherent, and comprehensive Schemes of Work and most importantly Programmes of Study are. They may not be as clear, comprehensive, or as coherent as they should be.

> **When there is an issue with pupil progress, nine times out of ten, start with the programme of study and the scheme of work.**
> **These will quickly tell you how organised the department is in relation to the comprehensive organisation, pace of delivery, and effective formative and summative assessment of the curriculum.**

■ From the data, gather further evidence to triangulate, support, and focus your lines of enquiry and inform the strengths to be celebrated and the issues to address.

To help prepare the best report on the exam results, explore what others have written or are doing. Cooper (2017), Gill (2017), and the Department for Education – DfE (2016a) offer some useful insights and a number of groups, including PiXL, the DfE, and exam boards on their websites, give some useful guidance. More information on these can be found in Chapter 15 at the end of this book. In addition, using online tools such as Survey Monkey or Google Forms enables you to efficiently evaluate your work with staff, students, and parents, saving you precious time.

After writing your report, use the following to check that you have covered these key points:

Analyse

■ Is your data reported against the school's (and local and national where available) three-year trend?

■ How well does your data compare to previous school and the latest local and national benchmarks?

■ What positive and less than positive messages about learning, teaching, and leadership come out of the data in the exam results?

■ What patterns about learning, teaching, and leadership are there in the data from the exam results?

Evaluate

■ What targets/goals were set to be achieved in relation to exam results and have these targets/goals been achieved, partially achieved, or not achieved?

- What went well and what could have been improved? Have you consulted with key staff involved in the process and enabled them to give their views?

- What do you understand to be the reasons behind any successes and any areas that were less successful in the exam results?

Action

- What follow-up actions need to be made, or key messages need to be communicated for staff, parents, Governors, and the local public as a result of your analysis/evaluation of the data?

- Which students have the potential for Oxbridge/Russell Group universities? Begin preparing applications.

Celebrate

- Arrange a suitable and appropriate method of celebrating the success of your results. Invite in ex-pupils to talk to staff. Write letters of appreciation to key teachers and leaders for their notable positive contribution.

- Publish a press release, social media posts, and an article for the school's newsletter/website with your good news. Make explicit the progress you are making as a school.

Celebrate more permanently!

- Utilise your wall space and your website – both are free! Displaying your success as a school through, for example, photographs of successful pupils, teams, destinations, or annotated work. This is therefore a free way to keep reinforcing the message that your school is successful.

Moments that count in September: Results

One particular year, the deputy head came into my Year 10 class and asked me if I were able to take a new pupil, just arrived from Japan, based on the (possibly flawed) understanding that being from Japan, she was likely to be musical. After a week of trying to teach music to our new pupil Suzie Takeda, and with no English understood by her and no Japanese understood by me, we called it a day in the GCSE Music class.

Fast forward 2 years and the first day back of school in September. Some half dozen pupils were brought into the first staff meeting of the year by the deputy head, all of whom had just received their results. They had been invited to give feedback to the staff about their experience at the school, in particular, in their final year. The line-up included Suzie Takeda. I uncharitably thought that this would be an interesting presentation given that, in my experience, Suzie could speak no English. When it came to her turn, Suzie made a beautiful presentation, spoken in perfect English, concluding with a thank you to the pupils and staff for their generosity, time, and support during her time at the school. After all the pupils in the line-up had left, the deputy head said to the staff "and I want you all to remember in particular, Suzie Takeda, because having joined the school 2 years ago unable to speak any English, she leaves the school with the second highest set of results in the year group. Testimony to her hard work, determination and being open to new experiences and an ability to get on with people; lessons there for some of the other pupils with whom we work". "Well", I thought, "that's told me".

Whilst for a school, the end of the summer holidays sees another set of exam results and another year done, for every pupil, the end of the summer holidays sees the end of that particular year of experiences and the passing (in both senses of the word) of those particular exams. For pupils like Suzie Takeda, this was a life-changing moment that saw her take her place within a new community and begin a new life. These are the moments that count; moments where schools must make a big effort to celebrate their pupils' exam results. For these pupils, this is a once-in-a-lifetime moment they will never forget and as such, it is incumbent on school leaders to celebrate with them and make these moments that count, unforgettable.

 (Senior leaders)   Pupil recruitment and destinations

Securing progress by knowing the strengths and unique selling points (USPs) of the school

Whether primary or secondary, before moving on from the results and into the rest of the school year, take a moment to consider the journey your pupils are making with you, where they are coming from and where they are going. To help cross-reference how successful pupil recruitment has been over the school year, the DfE and providers such as SIMS offer some useful insights and companies such as Education Advisers on their website give some useful guidance. More information on these can be found in Chapter 15 at the end of the book. In addition, using online tools such as Survey Monkey or Google Forms enables you to efficiently evaluate your work with students and staff, saving you precious time. After writing your report, use the following questions to check that you have covered key points.

Analyse

- Have you clearly presented the data on the areas/feeder schools of the pupils who are joining you and the secondary schools, universities, and employment destinations for those that are leaving?

- How does this data compare to the previous years and the latest local and national benchmarks?

- What positive and less than positive messages about learning, teaching, and leadership come out of the recruitment and destinations of this year's pupils?

- What patterns about learning, teaching, and leadership are there in the recruitment and destinations of this year's pupils?

Evaluate

- What targets/goals were set to be achieved in relation to the recruitment and destinations of this year's pupils and have these targets/goals been achieved, partially achieved, or not achieved?

- What went well and what could have been improved? Have you consulted with key staff involved in the process and enabled them to give their views in relation to the recruitment and destinations of this year's pupils?

- What do you understand to be the reasons behind any successes and any areas that were less successful in relation to pupil recruitment/pupil destinations?

Action

- What follow-up actions need to be made, or key messages communicated as a result of your analysis/evaluation?

Celebrate

- Celebrate all pupils and their achievements, whether significant progress, attainment, or achievement.

- What do the completed questionnaires/surveys by pupils joining/leaving the school say? Are there quotes that can be used to support and promote progress?

- With the pupils who are joining/leaving the school, are there any that may be willing to come and speak to staff, pupils, or parents about their journey, lessons learnt, and hopes and thoughts for and about the school?

(Senior leaders) **An improved working environment increases the chances of pupils achieving success**

By having an improved working environment, more pupils have the possibility of achieving success

For primary and secondary school leaders, to help cross-reference how successful the repairs and maintenance has been over the school year, the DfE (2016b) offers some useful insights and your Local Education Authority on their website gives some useful guidance. More information on these can be found in Chapter 15 at the end of this book. In addition, using online tools such as Survey Monkey or Google Forms with staff enables you to efficiently evaluate your work, saving you precious time. After writing your report/presentation about the repairs and maintenance of the school that have been completed over the holidays, use the following questions to check that you have covered these key points in your report:

Analyse

- What positive messages for learning, teaching, and leadership come out of the repairs and maintenance across the school?
- How will the work completed support greater progress in the school?
- What key messages come out of the repairs and maintenance across the school that pupils, teachers, and leaders need to hear?

Evaluate

- What targets/goals/actions were set to be achieved in relation to the repairs and maintenance programme and have these targets/goals been achieved, partially achieved, or not achieved?
- What went well and what could have been improved? Have you consulted with key staff involved in the process and enabled them to give their views in relation to the repairs and maintenance programme?
- What do you understand to be the reasons behind any successes and areas that were less successful in relation to the repairs and maintenance programme?

Action

- What follow-up actions need to be made/key messages need to be communicated as a result of your analysis/evaluation?

Celebrate

This is arguably as good as the school looks at the end of the summer holidays. Enjoy and use this moment to celebrate the great work that has been done over the summer.

■ Arrange a (virtual) tour of the school, post it on the school's website, and link this to social media posts.

■ Send thank you cards/make a presentation with the site team at the first staff meeting of the year.

■ Publish social media posts, a press release if significant building work has been completed, or have a major article for the school's newsletter/website published.

 (All leaders)   The integrated work of the school

Securing progress by implementing effective leadership, teaching, and learning strategies

In light of the results, whether primary or secondary, there may be some ramifications in relation to the school's budget, curriculum, class sizes, teaching, support staffing, and leadership. To help cross-reference how successful the integrated work has been over the school year, or for guidance as to how the school's practice might be improved, Salomon (2016) and Reynolds (2014) offer some useful insights and the DfE on their website give some useful guidance. More information on these can be found in Chapter 15 at the end of this book. In addition, using online tools such as Survey Monkey or Google Forms with the students and staff enables you to efficiently evaluate your work, saving you precious time. After writing your report, use the following questions to check that you have covered these key points:

Analyse

■ Is the impact of the latest recruitment numbers to the school clear on the school's budget, curriculum, class sizes, teaching, support staffing, and leadership?

■ How does this compare to previous years and the three-to-five-year strategic plan for the school?

■ What positive and less than positive messages about learning, teaching, and leadership come out of this?

■ What emerging patterns about learning, teaching, and leadership are there in this?

Evaluate

■ What targets/goals were set to be achieved in relation to the integrated framework and have these targets/goals been achieved, partially achieved, or not achieved?

■ What went well and what could have been improved? Have you consulted with key staff involved in the process and enabled them to give their views in relation to the school's budget, curriculum, class sizes, teaching, staffing, and leadership?

■ What are the reasons behind any successes and any areas that were less successful in this area?

Action

■ What follow-up actions related to learning, teaching, and leadership need to be made, or key messages communicated as a result of your analysis/ evaluation?

Celebrate

■ Send thank you cards/make a presentation with the relevant teams at the first staff meeting of the year to celebrate the increased efficient and effective working as a school.

■ Publish social media posts, a press release, or have a major article for the school's newsletter/website written to celebrate any significant progress that has been made in relation to the budget, school population, or curriculum.

 (All leaders) All statutory requirements are in place and live

All statutory requirements are in place

Before you get your team working, use the following to help check that you have covered all the key policies that are needed to ensure all statutory requirements are in place for the new year ahead. All are applicable to both primary and secondary schools, unless otherwise stated:

■ Administration and finance

■ Admissions

■ Assessment

■ Behaviour and attendance

- Curriculum

- Early years foundation stage (Primary)

- Governance

- Looked-after children

- Safeguarding children and young people

- Special educational/health needs (SEN Provision, including Educational Health Care Plans)

- Staff employment and teachers pay

- Schools and colleges careers guidance (Secondary)

In making your school policies available for your school community, a link to the government's list of statutory requirements can be found in Chapter 15 under Statutory Requirements to check you have done everything you need to ensure the school is fully compliant.

 (Senior leaders)   Staff/pupil induction successfully completed

All induction successfully completed

Whether a primary or secondary school, ensuring a smooth start to the year is in everyone's best interest. Having all the documentation and resources needed, right from the start, means everyone can get on with the job of delivering high-quality education from the outset. Before you get your induction team working, or you make your presentation to others, use the following to help check that you have covered all the actions that are needed for staff and pupil induction to be a success:

- Have you clearly articulated what you and others need to do, and when and where regarding induction?

- Have you clearly articulated how staff/pupils' work will benefit as a result of what you are asking people to do?

- What is the deadline for the work to be completed?

- What clear milestones are to be reached along the way?

- If this is additional to people's work, what should they do about covering their other work that is being missed?

- What should people do if there is a problem?

Here is a list of key information that needs to be in place from the start. A member of the Senior Leadership Team (SLT) should ensure that all of this information is ready, available, and accessible before the start of the school year. An electronic copy of this start of year checklist can be found and downloaded from the School Leader's Resources page at: www.schoolleaderdevelopment.com.

STAFF – START OF YEAR CHECKLIST (A-Z)	WHO TO SEE/ RESPONSIBILITY	LOCATION
Break and lunch arrangements		
Car parking information		
Child protection information		
Class lists		
Code of Conduct		
Computer password		
Computer systems login details		
Computer working		
Cover procedures		
Diary		
Duties schedule		
Email access		
Emergency telephone numbers		
ID card		
Interactive whiteboard (IWB) working		
Keys – to rooms/office		
Meetings schedule		
Photocopy number		
Pigeonhole		
Planner		
Policies		
Printer working		
Resources working		
Safeguarding		
School Calendar		
SEN information		
Staff Handbook		
Telephone access		
Telephone extensions list		
Timetable		
Union information		

PUPILS – START OF YEAR CHECKLIST (A-Z)	WHO TO SEE/ RESPONSIBILITY	LOCATION
Attendance expectations		
Behaviour expectations		
Break and lunch arrangements		

PUPILS – START OF YEAR CHECKLIST (A-Z)	WHO TO SEE/ RESPONSIBILITY	LOCATION
Computer passwords and logins		
Emails		
Emergency telephone numbers		
Equipment		
Exercise books and textbooks		
Homework		
ID card		
Internet usage		
Mobile telephones		
PE and sports kit		
Photocopying		
Printing		
Punctuality		
Pupil Charter		
Pupil Planner		
Rewards and sanctions		
Safeguarding		
School Calendar – key dates		
School Council information		
Security and lockers		
Timetable		
Tutor group information		
Uniform		

>>> **(All leaders)   Timetable/website/duties/routines in place**

Securing progress by knowing the school community works efficiently and effectively

Whether from a primary or secondary background, the infrastructure of the school is central to its effectiveness and is a key responsibility of the leadership of the school. Setting clear expectations right from the outset sets the tone for the year ahead. Clarifying with pupils, staff, and parents the expectations of key school activities ensures as smooth a start to the term and the school year for the whole school community as possible. Before you get your team working, press "send" on that email, or you make your presentation to others, use the following to help check that you have covered all the actions that are needed for the smooth running of the school to be a success:

 Be clear in articulating what you and others need to do and how to do it.

 Be clear in articulating how this work will benefit pupils.

 Be clear about what people should do if there is a problem.

Duties and routines include:

- **Absence and cover arrangements (teachers)**: What to do if staff are sick, who to call, what to do; this is a critical procedure to get clear and get right.

- **Absence and catching up on missed work (pupils)**: Again, what should the pupil and parents do if a pupil is sick, who to call, what to do; this is similarly, a critical procedure to get clear and get right.

- **Attendance**: Start and end times, the definition of "late" to school and procedures if staff/pupils are late.

- **Behaviour**: Posters and signage work well in clearly articulating what the expectations are with regards to behaviour and the commensurate rewards and sanctions.

- **Breaks and lunchtimes**: Clearly spell out where pupils and duty staff need to be/are allowed to go.

- **Complaints**: Clearly explain if things do not go as well as we would all like, what to do and who to see.

- **Finances**: Whether topping up lunch money or asking for petty cash to cover a moderate expense, it is important to clarify for staff, pupils, and parents the processes for paying in money or reclaiming expenses.

- **Lessons/registration/tutor time**: A presentation to express what the expectations are around entry to, structure of, and exit from lessons, registration, and tutor time helps create an orderly environment.

- **Lunch arrangements**: Clearly articulate (posters are invaluable here) how lunch is organised and who comes to lunch, and when.

- **Meetings**: What the meetings schedule is; who should be in attendance; where and when they take place; how agendas and minutes are created creates a sense of order and purpose to the other major area of schoolwork, outside of lessons.

- **Movement around school**: Again, posters and signage work well in clearly articulating what the expectations are when moving around school.

- **Timetable**: It is clear to everyone where they need to be and when. Nothing is omitted.

- **Trips and visits**: A letter to pupils and parents works well in clearly articulating what the expectations are with regards to processes, procedures, and expectations regarding trips and visits.

- **Website**: Clearly articulate with staff what information is needed for the website and how that is managed.

Moments that count throughout the year:
Leaders foster effective relationships

We all know that the secret of any relationship is an understanding of the dynamic; the differing personalities, particular preferences or dislikes, the relative strengths and weaknesses of each party, the potential ways that an individual will instigate, act, and respond. All of this is further complicated by the fact that relationships rarely develop along a straight trajectory nor at a constant pace. As I say to my students who are having friendship issues or in conflict with a member of staff: "Relationships are tough".

When you are a new leader then, the challenge is on to rapidly foster effective working relationships: if you are the Headteacher who is the new arrival, then the challenge is really on. As an existing member of an SLT which was joined by a new Assistant Head, Deputy Head, and Headteacher within a couple of years, I have experienced a number of moments that count which have skilfully fostered effective working relationships. An effective relationship has a common understanding, respect, and trust: Building this requires an investment of time, and this is where my new Headteacher began.

One week, the Head gave personal time to speak with each SLT member. They asked about my role, its form, function, purpose, its successes and challenges. This was an important first step in fostering the relationship, as it allowed me to express, critique, and confirm my own role in the SLT dynamic, receive affirmation and direction, and get to know my new team leader in an honest and open way. This one-to-one element of relationship maintenance has continued with each member of the SLT since the start.

Effective group relationships are fostered by creating shared experiences

A second moment that counted was when my new Headteacher, in their second year, reviewed the school mission statement. This activity allowed all of the senior team to express their educational opinions and principles: A vocal defining of the group's professional consciousness. Each person's contribution creating the new collective voice, which was then summarised in the words of the mission statement and owned by the team. This common direction of travel strengthened relationships.

Knowing when to reaffirm the group identity is a key to skilled leadership

A final moment that counted was provided by the Head this academic year. Covid restrictions had created an enforced, reductionist version of SLT interaction, consisting of tinny sound and small images on a computer screen, frozen any second according to the caprices of Wi-Fi connectivity. The potential dysconnectivity of SLT relationships in this situation was effectively disarmed by inviting the SLT to complete an online psychometric test. This produced an individualised list of character strengths: This was a guaranteed and timely boost to each member of the team to read a list of 24 personality positives about themselves.

> Buoyed by this initial affirmation of my best values, my top five positive attributes were collated with the top five values of each of my SLT colleagues, and the anonymised results presented at our next meeting. Playfully, we were invited to guess the owner of each set of words, which revealed the knowledge that colleagues had about one another, and understanding of each other's personalities and character. On a serious level, to see in the lists of my colleagues, the repeated mentions of words like "integrity", "honesty", "fairness", "teamwork", and "leadership" defined the collective professional morality and ability of the team and reaffirmed the relationships which ensure an effective working dynamic.
>
> Anon, Senior Leader

 (All leaders)   All policies go live and are implemented

Securing progress by ensuring that the education provided by you is compliant

If you have done all the preparation, this should be a simple and straightforward action. Putting the policies on the school's shared area, making them available to Governors, and signposting staff to them through the staff handbook are all useful and important actions. Regularly ensuring that the website has the correct policies available for parents and visitors to the website is key. A link to the government's expectations as a list of statutory policies can be found in Chapter 15 under "Policies". Once they have gone live, use the following to help check that all the correct policies are publicised on your school's website:

- School contact details
- Admission arrangements
- Ofsted reports
- Exam and assessment results
- Performance tables
- Curriculum
- Behaviour policy
- School complaints procedure
- Pupil premium
- Year 7 literacy and numeracy catch up premium
- PE and sport premium for primary schools

- Special Educational Needs and disability information
- Careers programme information
- Equality objectives
- Governors' information and duties
- Charging and remissions policies
- Values and ethos
- Requests for paper copies
- Financial information

 (All leaders) Arrange and send off examination appeals

Securing progress by securing the best results possible

For secondary schools, from earlier in the month, there may be exam results which, if below 1% or 2% of a grade level, can be appealed. With a tight deadline set by exam boards, the sooner this is dealt with, the sooner it gets resolved. Some parents, rather than the school, may also wish to appeal and so, starting this process early, as soon as pupils have returned and early expectations communicated, will help. When leading and managing the exam appeals process, use the following to help check that you have covered all bases before the pupils and parents walk through the door. Have you:

- Checked Ofqual, DfE, and Joint Council for Qualifications (JCQ) websites for the latest developments (see Chapter 15)?
- Trained key staff to support pupils and their families with an appeal?
- Decided your school's strategy for the releasing Centre Assessed Grades (CAG) and Rank Order (RO) results?
- Prepared to respond to subject access and Freedom of Information requests?
- Planned ahead to cover the various tasks and responsibilities?
- Considered the evidence the school will request from the examination boards?
- Prepared for potential complaints – have you a copy of the complaints procedures to hand?
- Planned Sixth Form Admissions appeals?
- Considered notifying insurers?
- Considered Serious Incident reports?

To help prepare the best examination appeals, explore what others have written or are doing. Salvato (2019) and the JCQ (2020) offer some useful insights and the DfE on their website gives some useful guidance. More information on these can be found in Chapter 15 at the end of this book. Also, use online tools such as Google Docs or Google Sheets to work on key documents or data concurrently with your team and ensure you work as effectively as possible.

>>> **(Senior leaders)   Assemblies and Inspiring Minds**

Securing progress through celebrating success, focusing improvement, and inspiring aspiration

For both primary and secondary schools, implementing an annual assemblies programme enables voices that may previously have been silent to be re-engaged and built into a coherent, considered programme, that is tied to the school's values/ethos and is inspiring and motivating. When writing your programme, consider using the following to help write or check your programme:

- Check literature and websites (see Chapter 15 and bibliography) to help create an assembly schedule.

- Create and publicise the schedule of assemblies/Inspiring Minds Programme for the term/year.

- Be clear in articulating what you and presenters/pupils/tutors/other staff/guests need to do to experience a successful assembly.

- Set clear deadlines for presentations to be completed.

- Model what a successful assembly looks like.

- Be clear about what people should do if there is a problem.

Here are some ideas to help assemblies be inspiring and motivational:

> **Guest speakers: Local dignitaries, MPs, community leaders, and religious leaders who can all bring the world in an inspiring way into the school.**
>
> **Pupil presentations: Have a rota of assemblies/presentations which pupils can prepare in advance/record and play at the appropriate time.**
>
> **Displays: Have an eye-catching display in the reception area of the inspiring people/messages from the pupils.**

An electronic copy of this assemblies calendar can be found and downloaded from the School Leader's Resources page at: www.schoolleaderdevelopment.com.

KEY ASSEMBLY DATES/THEMES

September
8th International Day of Democracy
9th First Aid Day
14th National Quiet Day
15th International Day of Peace
28th National Poetry Day
29th World Teacher's Day
Invitees: Local/celebrity politicians/poets

October
2nd Birthday – Gandhi
6th World Mental Health Day
16th World Food Day
16th Birthday – Oscar Wilde
25th Birthday – Picasso
31st Hallowe'en
Invitees: Local/celebrity artists

November
3rd World Science Day
7th Birthday – Marie Curie
9th World Freedom Day
10th Diwali
11th Remembrance Day
19th Anti-Bullying Week
24th National Tree Week
30th Self-Harm Awareness Day
Invitees: Local/celebrity religious leaders

December
1st World AIDS day
4th -10th Charities Week
8th Human Rights Day
Invitees: Local/celebrity charities

January
1st New Year's Day
4th Birthday – Isaac Newton
5th World Braille Day
8th Birthday – Stephen Hawking
19th Martin Luther King Day
26th International Customs Day
26th Education Week
27th Holocaust Memorial Day
Invitees: Local/celebrity teachers

February
4th World Cancer Day
7th Birthday – Charles Dickens
8th Safer Internet Day
9th Ash Wednesday/Social Justice Day
14th Valentine's Day
Invitees: Local/celebrity service men/women

March
1st St David's Day
3rd World Maths Day
4th World Book Day
5th International Women's Day
9th National Science and Engineering Week
11th Mother's Day
18th St Patrick's Day
Invitees: Local/celebrity scientists

April
1st April Fool's Day
20th National Volunteer Week
23rd St George's Day/Birthday
– Shakespeare
23rd World Book Day
27th RSPCA Week
Invitees: Local/celebrity authors

May
5th Deaf Awareness Week
18th International Children's Day
22nd Birthday – Buddha
Invitees: Local/celebrity sports men/women

June
1st World Environment and Oceans Day
8th Birthday – Tim Berners Lee
15th Refugee Week
17th Father's Day
22nd Birthday – HRH the Queen
23rd Birthday – Alan Turing
Invitees: Local/celebrity influential people

July
4th USA Independence Day
6th Birthday – Dalai Lama
14th Bastille Day
Invitees: Local/celebrity business leaders

(All leaders)   **Assessment programme in place**

Securing progress by having a way of assessing learning that is best practice and effective

For both primary and secondary schools, having a clear, effective assessment programme in place early sets the tone for the year ahead. Clarifying with pupils, staff, and parents the expectations of assessment ensures as smooth and consistent a start to the term and the school year for the whole school community. Before you press "Go", or you make your presentation to others, use the following to help check that you have covered all of the following points that are needed for the effective assessment of progress across the school and use these with staff in In-Service Education and Training (INSET)/CPD:

> Ingredients of a robust assessment programme to check include:
>
> - **Benchmarking**: This is usually the figure given based on a pupil's prior attainment.
> - **Ambitious targets**: How you set ambitious targets is up to each individual establishment. Most schools go with FFT 20, which means pupils aim to achieve similar results to the pupils attaining in the top 20% nationally.
> - A **clear and comprehensive curriculum**: Delivered through lessons, schemes of work, and programmes of study.
> - **Clear goals**: A clear understanding of what needs to be learnt by the end of each lesson, each scheme of work, and each programme of study.
> - **Assessment criteria**: explaining what is expected to achieve particular grades when assessing the learning of the curriculum.
> - **Assessment methodology**: A clear explanation of testing, whether *formative assessment for learning* or *summative assessment of learning* to inform and outline the rate of progress being made. This outlines how pupils receive feedback on their work. This also outlines the development of teacher, peer, and self-assessment during the modules being taught.
> - **Catch up and revision strategies**: These are strategies which would be deployed if the pupils weren't making sufficient progress and needed to catch up on previously missed work and revision to refresh previously learnt work.

| 👍 ⟳ ⟫⟫ | **(All leaders)** | **Update all plans and CPD** |

Securing progress by having improved learning due to improved teaching and leadership

Whether leading in a primary or secondary school, before updating the School/Faculty Improvement Plan, the SLT /Heads of Department need to **audit** their work first in light of the results achieved and work completed to date, where we are now in relation to previous results and inspection against each criterion. Once this audit is complete, the plan should **summarise** the current position, summarising each section, providing a summary overall, and where possible, indicating a summary for this year and over time, ideally a three-year trajectory.

To help prepare the best improvement plan, explore what others have written or are doing. Dunford (2016), the DfE (2019a), and Ofsted (2019b) offer some useful insights and The Key and the SSAT on their websites give some useful guidance. More information on these can be found in Chapter 15 at the end of this book. Also, use online tools such as Google Docs or Google Sheets to work on key documents or data concurrently with your team and ensure you work as effectively as possible. When writing your summary, consider using the following to help write or check your improvement and CPD plan:

All reporting should be clear as to what has improved/needs to be improved with supporting data. Specifically:

- Areas that are **going well** which should be maintained by sharing best practice in staff INSET/CPD.

- Areas that are **inconsistent**, where short-term improvements are needed to strengthen these areas.

- Areas that are significantly **underperforming**, where urgent transformative action is needed.

Any new intervention needs to be *sufficiently strong* to secure the changes/difference that needs to be made. Just doing something different may not be sufficient. Applying an intervention needs to deliver the changes required, with the ability to increase support if insufficient progress to the success criteria has been made.

The Improvement Plan identifies:

The clear goals needing to be achieved within a set time frame and identifies the broad actions related to pupils, staff, leadership, and others, including parents/Governors.

All actions should relate specifically to inspection criteria, with a clear outcome and impact (what will be in place once this action is completed (outcome) and what difference will this the outcome make (impact).

Questions to aid the completion of the School/ Faculty Improvement Plan (SIP / FIP)

▓ **Actions**: Who is going to do what by when?

▓ **Time frame**: When do changes start and finish?

▓ **Leadership**: Who is the lead person for the project?

▓ **Measure of success**: What is the measure of success to demonstrate that the work has been a success?

▓ **Target/success criteria**: What are the clear goals to be achieved?

▓ **Milestones**: What needs to be achieved and by when to show that progress is on track/sufficient?

▓ **Statutory reports**: Have you included the statutory areas of Behaviour/ Attendance/SEN (including Education and Health Care Plan – ECHPs)/ LAC (Looked After Children)/Behaviour/Attendance/Safeguarding/Careers in your report?

▓ Have you cross-checked your actions against the latest inspection criteria and that you are **Ofsted ready**?

Once the improvement plans have been completed, distribute these to your team to review clarity, consistency, and achievability and then begin!

An example of an action plan is included here and can also be found and downloaded from the School Leader's Resources page at: www.schoolleaderdev elopment.com:

INSPECTION			SCHOOL DEVELOPMENT		
Area	Criteria	Related criteria	Lead	Focus and success criteria	Outcome and impact
Overall effectiveness	1.1 1.2	1.4e 2.1a 2.14 2.2n 2.3b/c/e 2.4/e	Headteacher (HT)/SLT/ Head of Department (HOD)	School/ Department Improvement Plans are up to date and communicated to all stakeholders	A school improvement action plan to demonstrate school is consistently "Good". Impact: Consistent improvement in practice across every area of the school leading to increases in achievement for all pupils
Leadership and management	2.2e	2.2h 3.1a/b/c 3.2a/b/c3.2e/g 3.3a/b/c3.3d/g 3.9a/b 6.5a/b	HT/SLT/HOD	Monitoring and tracking of teaching and learning is up to date and communicated to all stakeholders	Teaching and learning improve in all subjects. Impact: Outstanding teaching leading to outstanding learning and achievement.
Teaching and Learning	3.2d	3.5a 3.8 3.10a	SLT/HOD/ Teachers	Assessment of work is consistent across all subjects	Regular monitoring of pupils' written work, with written feedback and re-drafting of work. Impact: Consistently high standard of pupils' work in books across all year groups and faculties.
Behaviour and welfare	4.1c	4.1d 4.5b	SLT/Head of Year (HOY)/ Tutors	Quality assurance programme in place for behaviour secures improvement in behaviour for all year groups	All pupils show increase in positive behaviour and reduction in negative behaviour. Impact: Pupils feel part of a caring community and work is done in a calm business-like environment.
Outcomes	5.1b	5.2a 5.5a/b 5.6 6.5b	HT/SLT/HOD	Intervention Programme and Plan of Action in place and reviewed regularly	All underachieving pupils improve and achieve their target grades. Impact: Consistent high-quality education across all year groups and faculties.

(All leaders)   Agree all quality assurance procedures

Securing progress by having leadership and teaching that has been checked by others

Whether in a primary or secondary school setting, having reviewed the old and written the new School/Faculty Improvement Plan, it should be clear as to what school improvement actions need to be done and by when, but who is going to quality assure that work? Many schools can fall into the trap of expecting leaders to get on with the job, needing no support or checks to ensure the quality of the work is sufficiently high. However, with the day-to-day work of teachers and leaders critical to the success of the school, it is prudent to have internal checks (other leaders/Governors) and external checks Multi-Academy Trust (MAT), Local Education Authority (LEA), school improvement consultants) on that work. Agreeing in advance what that checking looks like, the cost (time/energy/money) and impact it needs to have will help ensure there are no nasty surprises and/ or disappointments later in the year. Quality assurance by internal and external agencies can take many forms. Here are a few:

- Checking the work of leadership: Audit of progress to date – joint learning walks

- Checking the work of leadership: Monitoring and tracking – joint scrutiny of spreadsheets, data analysis, patterns

- Checking the quality of support and progress: Joint lesson observations and staff/student feedback

- Checking the impact of leadership: Joint document scrutiny/book looks/work scrutinies

- Evaluating the work of leadership: Individual or group staff/student interviews, questionnaire responses

Once the decisions have been made as to the sort of quality assurance which will work best for the department/school, consider the following points to help create and structure your quality assurance programme:

- Are all the resources needed to do the quality assurance in place?

- Is everyone sufficiently skilled at quality assurance to do the work you want them to do?

- Have you cross-checked your actions against the latest inspection criteria and that you are Ofsted ready?

> If the answer is no to the above, consider delaying the start of any quality assurance work until there are sufficient resources/staff are sufficiently trained and skilled in what to do.

Once resources are sufficient, and staff are sufficiently skilled:

- Be clear in articulating what you and others need to do and how to do it as regards quality assurance.

- Be clear in articulating how a quality assurance programme will benefit pupils.

- Set clear deadlines for the work to be completed.

- Set clear milestones to be reached along the way.

- Model what success looks like. To what extent is best practice being shared, e.g. in staff INSET/CPD?

- Be clear about what people should do if there is a problem.

To help prepare the best quality assurance programme, explore what others have written or are doing. Ofsted (2019a) offer some useful insights and Ofsted, The Key, and your Local Education Authority on their websites give some useful guidance. More information on these can be found in Chapter 15 at the end of this book. Also, use online tools such as Google Docs or Google Sheets to work on key documents or data concurrently with your team and ensure you work as effectively as possible.

 (Senior leaders)   Finalise and implement the budget

Securing progress through implementing the most efficient and effective budget

Having had the results in, got the school year underway, and identified the course of action for the rest of the year, the financial sails need to be trimmed and the budget reviewed in light of these. For both primary and secondary schools, when updating your financial plans, consider using the following to help write or check your programme:

- Liaise initially with Governors, particularly the Chair of the Finance committee and Chair of Governors if some difficult financial decisions need to be made. Tease these through with the senior leadership team if necessary.

■ Communicate the final decisions to staff as to the most effective/appropriate financial way forwards for the school, minimising as far as possible any negative impact on the progress of the pupils.

■ For any difficult news, be thoroughly prepared with the relevant HR guidance.

This is the last of the actions influenced by previous work and from this point forwards, the course for the year ahead is set.

 (All leaders) Successfully carry out Open Evening / Week

Securing progress by reinforcing the unique successes of your department/school

---

This is the jewel-in-the-crown event of the year and, in my experience, where the school sparkles. However, it is also high risk. I have heard of some headteachers, in a bid to outdo local competition, taking risks that failed and paid a heavy price with pupil recruitment as a result. So, show your department or your school off at their best, but do not try to be something you are not. Equally, we live in a world which functions increasingly through technology. Think of it as putting on a West End musical, with a cast of hundreds. Getting every detail, including key messages and the practicalities such as PowerPoints, sound, lighting, and logistics right will maximise the impact of such an important part of the school calendar. When writing your plan of action for Open Evening in September or October for Reception and Key Stage 3, or in January for Key Stage 5, consider using the following to help write or check your plan:

■ Be clear in articulating what you and others need to do and how to do it.

■ Be clear in articulating how this work will benefit pupils.

■ Set a clear deadline for the work to be completed.

■ Set clear milestones to be reached along the way.

■ Model what success looks like. To what extent is best practice being shared, e.g. in staff INSET/CPD?

■ Be clear about what people should do if there is a problem.

An electronic copy of the following Open Evening checklist can be found and downloaded from the School Leader's Resources page at: www.schoolleaderdev elopment.com to help prepare what should be the event of the year!

Open Day/Evening checklist

TO DO	TIMING	ACTION BY	COMPLETE
Admission criteria	3 months in advance		
Prospectus	3 months in advance		
Photos/promotional video	3 months in advance		
Book uniform company	3 months in advance		
New signage arranged where necessary	6 weeks before		
Posters created and sent to printers	1 month in advance		
Information to parents/feeder schools	1 month in advance		
Projector (PowerPoint) check	1 month in advance		
Stage lighting/Sound check	1 month in advance		
Exam Results posters	3 weeks before		
Display board organisation	3 weeks before		
Material ordering system	3 weeks before		
Prefects and guides	3 weeks before		
Music	3 weeks before		
Parents' Information Pack	3 weeks before		
Governors/PTA	3 weeks before		
Walk around site	3 weeks before		
Car parking	2 weeks before		
Notification of day pattern	2 weeks before		
Routes	2 weeks before		
Organise special staff briefing	2 weeks before		
Notes for staff	2 weeks before		
Letters to parents/local residents	2 weeks before		
Proforma regarding lunch/early closing	2 weeks before		
Flowers ordered	1 week before		
Classroom notice boards updated	1 week before		
Corridor notice boards	1 week before		
Classroom activities	1 week before		
Cleaning arrangements	1 week before		
Staff car parking	1 week before		
OFSTED quotes/results displayed	1 week before		
Catering on the day	1 week before		
Photographing the evening	1 week before		
Briefing of whole school	1 week before		
Staff – confirmation of expectations	1 week before		
HT speech check	Day before		
Prefect/guides briefing	Day before		
Notices for entrance	Day before		
Evaluation form created and copied	Day before		
Distribute display boards	On the day		
Organise handouts on tables	On the day		
Site check	On the day		
Supervision of detention	On the day		
Food and drink for staff	On the day		
Coffee/biscuits (urns)	On the day		
Name badges	On the day		
Pastoral care	On the day		
Door wedges	On the day		
Final prefects/guides briefing	On the day		
Show time!			
Welcome Pack and register	During the event		
Manage any special requirements	During the event		
Tickets for speeches	During the event		
Ring bells for speeches	During the event		

Moments that count in September and October: Open Evening

One particular Open Evening, the event had started, and having a new head-teacher, the school hall was full of anticipatory parents and restless children, keen to see the new regime and what improvements were going to be made in the years to come. With the hall brimming and a stage bedecked with flowers and model pupils all prepared and on show, the new headteacher entered.

As he mounted the stairs to the stage, he managed to dislodge his lapel microphone, so that when he took to the podium, a warm welcome was delivered with a loud rustling sound. He carried on. However, it was increasingly clear that the scraping noise accompanying his speech was not going to go away. After a couple of sentences, he stopped and tried to correct the microphone, in full view of the packed audience. As he tried to fix it to his lapel, he made matters worse by managing to drop the radio microphone onto the floor. Picking it up while muttering, amplified for all to hear, he replaced the microphone, clipped it back into place and finally offered a thunderously warm welcome to the school! However, the moment was lost. The prospective parents and pupils had witnessed less of a Headteacher's Open Evening opening speech, but more of a 30-second comedic soliloquy, with any gravitas or credibility lost. Subsequent to this, new pupil choices to the school dropped, with significant ramifications for the budget and staffing for the next five years.

> Open Evening is a key moment that literally counts, the importance of which we must never forget.
> Open Evening is a show, and like any West End show, must be note perfect from start to finish.
> Get it right and watch the numbers go up! Get it wrong and the numbers can just as easily go down.

 (All leaders)   Complete all performance appraisals

Securing progress by holding all staff to account for their work

Performance appraisal is a statutory requirement for all staff working in primary or secondary education and is used to ensure consistent good practice. It is the process whereby a school formally reviews its work. The objectives set are meant to be rigorous, challenging, achievable, time-bound, fair, and equitable in relation to teachers and support staff with similar roles/responsibilities and experience. They also take account of the member of staff's professional aspirations and any relevant pay progression criteria. Objectives should be such that, if they are achieved, they contribute to improving the progress of pupils at the school.

All staff, including the Headteacher, will usually have approximately three objectives. Ahead of actioning work on performance appraisal with the school/ your team, spend a short time preparing the groundwork:

- What needs to happen with regards to performance appraisal, and by when and by whom?

- What changes may have happened since last year that need to be considered/ addressed?

- Save time: Get copies/model examples of what you want and amend them to what you need.

Performance appraisal is evidence-based on a number of factors:

Whether performance management/appraisal objectives set a year ago were met

Whether Teaching Standards were met

Lesson observations

Quality of teaching (including marking, outcomes for pupils) over the previous year

---

To help prepare an effective performance appraisal process, explore what others have written or are doing. The DfE (2019b, 2019c, and 2019e) offer some useful insights and The Key and Blue Sky on their websites give some useful guidance. More information on these can be found in Chapter 15 at the end of this book. Also, use online tools such as Google Docs or Google Sheets to work on key documents or data concurrently with your team and ensure you work as effectively as possible.

 (Senior leaders) Confirm admissions arrangements

Securing progress by clarifying the success and growth of the school

Whether for primary schools with Reception this month and in January, or for secondary schools with Year 7, this is usually a fairly straightforward activity, confirming with the government or LEA, the pupil admission numbers for the next year. However, occasionally, numbers may need to go up or down and so more detailed arrangements need to be in place. Ahead of actioning work on admission arrangements, spend a short time preparing the groundwork. To help you with this, explore what others have written or are doing. Offenberg (2004) offers some useful insights and the DfE and your Local Education Authority on their websites give some useful guidance. More information on these can be found in Chapter 15 at the end of this book. In confirming admission arrangements, ensure you have clear answers to the following:

■ Who needs to be involved/consulted at the various stages of confirming admission arrangements?

■ Are you clear and have you communicated to relevant staff what needs to happen, and by when and by whom?

■ What are the key messages that need to be communicated?

■ Propose the best: Provide a proposal that incorporates research and shares best practice in what you do, e.g. in staff INSET/CPD.

■ Keep it flexible: Once your proposal is live, welcome feedback on what is going well and how it could be improved further.

 (All leaders) Prepare all follow-up procedures

Securing progress by not letting anyone achieve anything less than their best

The general expectation of a school is that every pupil should be achieving their best. Using a number of alternative measures available to schools (for example, FFT 20), every school predicts a child to achieve. However, the reality is that at times, some pupils may underachieve in their progress initially for three broad reasons: Absence from class, an inability to answer questions, or an inability to sufficiently complete work. Each of these, whilst producing the same result (underachievement), requires slightly different management.

ISSUE	SOLUTION	METHOD
Absence from lessons	Complete the missed work after school	Online work/Catch up programme
Inability to answer questions	Revision/exam practice/ targeted intervention	Revision groups/practice tests/ study-buddy
Insufficient work completed	Opportunities to catch up	Catch up programme/one-to-one support/small group work

Having a strong programme of general support available to them ensures that most pupils do not slip too far behind and continue to make sufficient progress (see table above). For secondary schools, to help prepare the best catch up and revision programmes, explore what others have written or are doing. Coates (2015) offers some useful insights and there are a number of excellent websites which give some really useful guidance and support. More information on these can be found in Chapter 15 at the end of this book. Also, use online tools such as Google Docs or Google Sheets to work effectively on key documents or data concurrently with your team. For primary schools, these can be used to support your catch up in February/March.

Also, use the following checklist to check that you are supporting all pupils to achieve their potential:

- This month, have you checked that pupils with more than two days absence have completed all missed work?
- In your schemes of work, have you built in time to revise and test current and previously learnt work?
- For pupils who need additional support to catch up with their classwork or coursework, have you put a schedule of support in place and communicated this to staff, pupils, and parents?

If underachievement continues to be evident in a number of subjects, or with a number of pupils in the same class, a plan of action must be implemented and followed. An analysis of the data may identify patterns in these categories:

- **By pupil**: Similar issues for a pupil in multiple subjects.

- **By teacher**: Similar issues for multiple pupils in one subject.

- **By leader**: Similar issues for multiple teachers/subjects in one faculty area.

- **Anomalies**: Any outliers that do not fit into any of the categories above.

Prioritisation for support should be done through identifying which issues are the most urgent; the most important; have the most impact; or are the most complex. See October for a more detailed explanation of this. A **support plan lasting between four to six weeks should be discussed and agreed** (see overleaf for an example), with progress reviewed at the end for the following:

- **Pupil support (individuals)**

- **Pupil support (target groups)**

- **Teacher support**

- **Leader support**

An electronic copy of an individual support plan can also be downloaded from the School Leader's Resources page at: www.schoolleaderdevelopment.com.

Individual support plan: Improving achievement

Name:
Form:

	Date	Review date	Staff involved
Meeting 1			
Meeting 2			
Meeting 3			

Reasons for poor achievement	**Targets to improve achievement**
▪ ▪ ▪	▪ ▪ ▪
Agreed timetable/subjects	**Pupil strategies to improve achievement**
▪ ▪ ▪	▪ ▪ ▪
School strategies to improve achievement	**Parent strategies to improve achievement**
▪ ▪ ▪	▪ ▪ ▪
Signed (pupil):	**Date:**
Signed (guardian):	**Date:**
Signed (school):	**Date:**

**(All leaders)   Prepare completion of
the Census**

Securing progress by ensuring everyone has the most up-to-date information on pupils

Whether you lead in a primary or secondary school, this is a highly complex activity, with a large amount of data gathered from many people. An early start on reading through the requirements and mobilising the key staff sooner rather than later will help the process go as smoothly as possible. To help complete the census as efficiently as possible, explore what others have written or are doing. The DfE (2020c) offer some useful insights and both the DfE and your Local Education Authority on their website give some useful guidance. More information on these can be found in Chapter 15 at the end of this book. Also, use online tools such as Google Docs or Google Sheets to work on key documents or data concurrently with your team and ensure you work as effectively as possible. In addition, before you prepare the census, ensure you can clearly answer the following:

▨   Who needs to be involved/consulted at the various stages?

▨   Are you clear and have communicated to relevant staff what needs to happen, and by when and by whom?

▨   What are the biggest challenges that lie ahead and how are those challenges going to be met?

▨   What are the key messages that need to be communicated?

▨   Keep it flexible: Once your proposal is live, welcome feedback on what is going well and how it could be improved further.

 (Senior leaders)   Celebrate the end and start of terms

Securing progress by understanding the effective processes and procedures in the school

For both primary and secondary schools, so that progress is made with timetabling, examination appeals (secondary schools), and induction next year, consider an evaluation of these processes for this year. Evaluate them by ensuring that all people involved in them (pupils, staff, parents, support staff) have an opportunity to feedback and give their views as to what they thought went well and what could have been improved. This should feed into your report to others. Before reporting on how well the start of the year went, use the following questions to check that you have covered these key points.

Analyse

- What positive messages and key learning, particularly related to learning, teaching, and leadership come out of the start of the year?

- What patterns are there and what are the ramifications of these patterns?

Evaluate

- Have you consulted with key staff involved in the process and enabled them to give their views as to what they thought went well and what could have been improved in relation to the start of the year?

- What do you understand to be the reasons behind any successes and any areas that were less successful at the start of the year?

Action

- What follow-up actions need to be made/key messages need to be communicated as a result of your analysis/evaluation?

Celebrate

- Arrange a suitable and appropriate method of celebrating success. Write letters of appreciation to key teachers and leaders for their notable positive contribution.

- Publish social media posts, a press release, and an article for the school's newsletter/website with your good news.

 (All leaders)   Evaluate and celebrate duties and routines

Securing progress by understanding the effective processes and procedures in the school

---

The school year, now fully underway, means an opportunity to review the routines that are in place and how effective and fit for purpose they are. In a similar way to the one-off events such as induction, evaluate the school's ongoing duties and routines by ensuring that all people involved in the process (pupils, staff, parents, support staff) have an opportunity to feedback and give their views as to what they thought went well and what could have been improved. This should feed into your report to others. Use the following to help support your feedback:

Analyse

- What positive messages and key learning, particularly related to learning, teaching, and leadership come out of the way the school has settled into the new routines?

■ What patterns are there in these messages and what are the ramifications of these patterns?

Evaluate

■ Have you consulted with key staff involved in the process and enabled them to give their views as to what they thought went well and what could have been improved in relation to duties and the new school routines?

■ What do you understand to be the reasons behind any successes and any areas that were less successful to the duties and new school routines?

Action

■ What follow-up actions need to be made/key messages need to be communicated as a result of your analysis/evaluation?

Celebrate

Effective routines deserve to be recognised and acknowledged. Use the following to help you craft an effective message of gratitude to staff, students, and parents for their work on helping create a calm and purposeful school.

■ Applaud that the school has settled into a good working rhythm.

■ Do not forget to celebrate! Arrange a method of celebrating success: An email or letter to pupils, parents, and staff, or message in the school's bulletin.

■ Create an opportunity to celebrate your school's success and make explicit the progress you are making as a school.

■ Celebrate more permanently: Wall space and your website are free! Displaying certain routines is a free way to keep reinforcing key messages and that your school is successful. Therefore, ensure the wall space in your school is used to full effect.

Summary and checklist for September

LEADER ACTION	FOCUS	SENIOR LEADERS	MIDDLE LEADERS
Evaluate and celebrate	Annual exam/test results		
	Pupil recruitment and destinations		▓
	Repairs/maintenance		▓
	The integrated work of the school		
Action	All statutory requirements are in place and live		▓
	Staff/pupil induction		
	Implement start of year arrangements/routines/timetable/website		
	Implement policies		
	Examination appeals		
	Implement Assemblies and Inspiring Minds Programme		▓
	Implement Assessment programme		
	Finalise and implement FIP/SIP/SEF, and CPD programme		
	Implement a revised budget plan		
	Open Evening/Week and update displays		▓
Arrange	Agree internal and external quality assurance (QA)		▓
	Performance appraisal and pay		
	Admissions arrangements		
	Coursework, Catch Up, and Revision programme format		
	Census		
Evaluate and celebrate	Timetable, appeals, induction/start of year	▓	▓
	Duties and routines		

October

October marks the end of the honeymoon period when school systems start to be tested.

It is also the month when data starts to arrive, providing initial glimpses of the potential successes and challenges that lie ahead.

October needs to be experienced with balance and resolve.

DOI: 10.4324/9781003129691-3

Introduction: October

October provides an opportunity to identify how well initial changes are taking place. It is also the first month to check the pace of progress in teaching and learning as initial data starts to emerge, indicating how well lessons to date have been learnt. The following strategies are for both senior and middle leaders to use at either the whole school or the department level, unless otherwise stated. Here is what lies ahead in October.

OCTOBER SUMMARY		
KEY		
👍 Action that evaluates and celebrates previous work	》》 Action that supports current work	⟳ Action that prepares future work
Statutory activity (higher priority)		**Non-statutory activity (lower priority)**
Action	*Leaders*	*School Focus for October*
👍	All leaders	Evaluate Open Evening and Open Week
》》	All leaders	Complete and return the Autumn term census
》》	Middle leaders	Set up Schemes of Work for Autumn 2
》》	All leaders	Implement Performance Appraisal/Pay Review
》》	All leaders	Monitoring and Tracking for Autumn in place
》》	All leaders	Implement Coursework, Catch Up, and Revision programmes
》》	All leaders	Quality assurance – Autumn 1 programme starts
》》	Senior leaders	Confirm admissions arrangements and pupil numbers
》》	All leaders	Update plans/School Evaluation Form (SEF) and continuing professional development (CPD) in light of first round of data
⟳	Senior leaders	Prepare surveys created for parents/staff and pupils
⟳	All leaders	Parents' Evenings arrangements agreed and arranged
⟳	Senior leaders	Pupil recruitment processes confirmed
⟳	Senior leaders	Integrated Framework initially considered

As October starts, create an opportunity at your next leadership team/department meeting to discuss the following standing agenda items:

- **Staffing and safeguarding**: Are there any staffing and/or safeguarding concerns to be urgently addressed this month?

- **Calendar**: Are there any pinch points this month which need to be carefully managed beforehand?

- **Trips and school activities**: Are there any trips or large group activities this month which need to be carefully managed?

- **Website and communications**: Is the website up to date and are parents/pupils/ staff clear about what is happening this month? Is there robust, challenging, and engaging online work available for pupils to complete if needed?

- **Inspection ready**: Which areas need addressing this month to ensure we are on track with our work?

The rationale for the other actions taking place this month, and in this order, include that an action is *more important* or needs doing *more urgently*, has a higher priority and therefore comes earlier in the month and vice versa. An action may be *part of a process* and so must happen before one action, but after another. Also, certain actions are *fixed* to events outside of the school's control and so these actions are tied to a particular date in the calendar (for example, external exams) or are actions *related to a fixed* event. Thus, an evaluation and celebration of the Open Evening and Open Week must take place in early October after the Open Evening and Open Week have come to a close.

Having got September wrapped up, the necessary work for October can begin. First off is the all-important autumn term census. This is a complex piece of work, so the sooner it begins, the sooner any issues can be resolved, and the census completed and returned on time. To proactively manage the team's stress and workload, Heads of Department can prepare in advance (where does the time go?) their schemes of work for teaching and learning after the October half term. In early October we can also begin and follow through to conclusion the Performance Appraisal process and any pay recommendations, as well as action a group of activities related to teaching and learning, including the setting up of the first round of monitoring and tracking with the subsequent coursework follow up, catch up, and revision activities. This informs the necessary internal and external quality assurance of the school's work, especially with new staff and beginner teachers. With the end of October comes provisional confirmation of pupil numbers into Year 7 and the need to confirm admission arrangements. Finally, in light of the first round of data, performance appraisals and the confirmation of potential pupil numbers it is possible to complete the first analysis and celebration of positive data and updating the SEF, improvement plans, and CPD programme.

Having had the school settle into some routines is as good a time as any to take the temperature, so to speak, and put out a review through a survey to pupils, parents, and staff as to their experience of the school since the start of term, enabling leaders to review and prepare effective parents' evenings. Following the Open Evening and having some idea of the potential recruitment to Year 7, leaders can now start looking at the recruitment and leaving processes and procedures with information from pupil and parent surveys addressed ahead of recruitment packs being written. All this acts as the catalyst to set the ball rolling and begin the consultation on the new integrated framework; the curriculum, class sizes, finances, and staffing for the next academic year.

The end of October brings half term and the opportunity for a much-deserved break! Here are the activities for October in more detail.

 (All leaders)　　　　**Open Evening and Open Week**

Securing progress by knowing the strengths of the school and celebrating them

Following on from one of the high points of the year, take a moment to consider the work you are doing in your department/school and the journey you are making. After writing your report on the lessons learnt from Open Evening and the Open Week, use the following questions to check that you have covered these key points.

Analyse

- Report your data from the feedback from staff, parents, and pupils who are potentially joining you and the potential changes that these indicate.

- How does this data compare to previous years, and the latest local and national benchmarks?

- What positive and less than positive messages about learning, teaching, and leadership come out of the Open Evening/Open Week to take on board and learn/change?

Evaluate

- What targets/goals were set to be achieved in relation to Open Evening/ the Open Week and have these targets/goals been achieved, partially achieved, or not achieved?

- What went well and what could have been improved? Have you consulted with key staff involved in the process and enabled them to give their views?

■ What do you understand to be the reasons behind any successes and any areas that were less successful in relation to Open Evening and the Open Week?

Action

■ What follow-up actions need to be made/key messages need to be communicated as a result of your analysis/evaluation?

Celebrate

Before moving on from Open Evening, spend a moment to recognise the great effort that went into a great evening.

■ Applaud that the school has pulled out all the stops and shown the school at their absolute best.

■ Arrange a method of celebrating success: Boxes of chocolates, cakes, an email or letter to pupils, parents, and staff, or message in the school's bulletin.

■ Upload any photographs and videos from the evening and create a "Welcome to the school" video for use with pupils who may be joining the school during the year.

Moments that count throughout the year: Respond; don't react

As an experienced Deputy Headteacher who has led various areas within senior leadership, you would have thought there would be little that I hadn't seen or heard before. Enter a global pandemic unlike anything seen in a generation and being asked to lead on navigating an entire school community through endless government guidance, government U-turns, risk assessments, exit plans into lockdown, reintegration plans out of lockdown, setting up a medical grade testing centre, planning the logistics for delivering 3000 Covid tests on site before organising the distribution of endless home testing ... and on and on.

In the occasional fleeting moments when I get the time to reflect on what has been the most challenging period of my career, yet also the most inspiring, what have I learnt? I've learnt that it's important to make sure you respond and communicate rather than react. Reaction is natural, as is our desire to make things okay for our staff, students, and parents, and the pressure to do so as soon as possible. This, coupled with the misconception that we somehow have an insight or secret government hotline into what will happen next creates an overwhelming sense of urgency!

There was a seminal moment after spending hours on a whole school risk assessment for the return to school after the first COVID lockdown, only to be issued with a local authority standardised framework that had to be used by all! Despite my frustration, I threw myself into the task and was making good progress when said framework "version 2" landed, with a whole new sequence and layout, thus nullifying any potential for cut and paste. This is when I realised I/we had reacted too soon; we should have waited, reflected, researched, and most of all, stolen other people's good ideas! Don't get me wrong, I am not advocating hesitancy or procrastination here, sometimes you have to move quickly to reassure your community. But sometimes, that security comes from the knowledge that your leaders have the strength of character and foresight to pause, and think, before jumping through the latest hoop or most recent trend.

Doing something well once is not only more efficient but also more reassuring for those who are looking to you to lead them through challenging times. You might get to the "Gala Ball" quicker in a convertible sports car, but you gain just as much attention pulling up in a limousine and exiting elegantly with not a hair out of place!

Dan Smith, Deputy Headteacher

 (All leaders) Complete the autumn term census

Securing progress by ensuring everyone has the most up-to-date information on pupils

As you may have gathered, this is a highly complex activity, with a large amount of data needing to be gathered from many people. An early start on reading through the requirements and mobilising the key staff sooner rather than later should have helped this first run go as smoothly as possible. Ahead of actioning work on the census, spend a short time preparing the groundwork, or checking the completion of it, with a small but important action plan:

- Consult the latest guidance on the census (see Chapter 15 for useful websites).

- Who needs to be involved/consulted at the various stages?

- Are you clear and have you communicated to relevant staff what needs to happen, and by when and by whom?

- What are the biggest challenges that lie ahead and how are those challenges going to be met?

- What are the key messages that need to be communicated to staff, leaders, and Governors?

■ Keep it flexible: Once your proposal is live, welcome feedback on what is going well and how it could be improved further.

> **>>> (Middle leaders)   Update Schemes of Work for Autumn 2**
>
> *Securing progress by providing a comprehensive, clear, and achievable curriculum*

Just like taking your pupils on a long journey to successfully reach the top of a mountain, progress needs careful planning to make sure the path taken is manageable and the goal is achieved on time.

Clear Scheme of Work aim:

By the end of this topic, you will have successfully completed your 1000-word essay on Health and Fitness.

Whether in a primary or secondary setting, as you review/prepare your scheme of work for the end of the autumn term, use the following to check it is as good as it can be:

■ Are the **aims** of the scheme of work and each lesson **realistically high**, **clearly articulated**, and **ordered coherently** so progress over the scheme of work is **explicit**?

■ Is the work to be completed **manageable, challenging**, and **consistently focused on pupil learning**?

■ Is there explicit **progression in understanding** from description and facts to analysis and reasoning?

■ Is there a clear **increase in the challenge/complexity of knowledge and skills** being learnt?

■ Is the work expected to be completed **increasingly longer and harder**?

■ Are activities progressing **from the class/group** to the **individual** over time and **includes homework**?

■ Is **assessment for learning built into each lesson** and does it move **from informal to formal assessment**?

■ What **provisions are in place** should anyone fall behind, or finish sooner than expected?

> **⟫⟫⟫** **(All leaders)** **Implement performance appraisals**
>
> *Securing progress by holding all staff to account for their work*

Having set up the performance appraisal process, has it been implemented as well as you would have hoped? Now it is time to check. Here are a few suggestions to help:

▪ Have you clearly articulated what you and others need to do, and when and where regarding performance appraisal?

▪ What is the deadline for the reviews to be completed?

▪ What clear milestones are to be reached (and communicated) along the way?

▪ Monitoring – having a tracking spreadsheet clearly identifying the staff, the paperwork they have received, and the deadline dates for the various stages of the process will help you keep track and in control of a very wide-ranging process.

---

1. All paperwork out (by the end of September)

2. All performance review meetings scheduled (first two weeks in October)

3. All completed and signed performance reviews returned (first two weeks in October)

4. Any incorrectly completed forms have been returned for correction (first two weeks in October)

5. All forms to the Headteacher/Principal for review and signature (third week in October)

6. Confirmatory letters to all staff as to the performance and pay conclusions (fourth week in October)

7. A summary report for the Senior Leadership Team (SLT) and Governors drafted, including whole school CPD recommendations (first week in November)

All of this is time-consuming and therefore ensuring each step is rigorously followed up, the sooner the completion of each stage of the process.

(All leaders)   Monitoring and Tracking for Autumn is in place

Securing success by routinely checking that everyone is making expected progress

Whatever our work as a primary or secondary school leader, there will be a need to observe the areas over which you lead and report on progress. Here are some questions to help ensure your monitoring tracking is as rigorous as it needs to be:

▧ Have you clearly articulated what you and others need to do, and when and where regarding monitoring and tracking teaching and learning?

▧ Have you clearly articulated how staff/pupils' work will benefit as a result of what you are asking people to do?

▧ What are the key deadlines for the work to be completed by?

▧ What should people do if there is a problem?

> **Keeping a file of evidence to also offer as case studies or examples of work will be necessary.**
>
> **A logical, easy-to-use, and frequently updated filing system is key.**
>
> **Having easy-to-use, reliable methods to gather clear, comprehensive evidence is also key.**
>
> **Either way, set up and regularly update a spreadsheet to gather and analyse key data.**

The following are critical to any data analysis and therefore any monitoring and tracking. These can be used as headings to structure your monitoring and tracking data sheet:

▧ **Target**: What is the single, clear target you are aiming to achieve?

▧ **Local/national benchmarks**: what is the single, clear target achieved locally/nationally?

▧ **Measure of success**: What are you measuring to show success?

▧ **Time frame**: What time frame is in place for your project to be a success?

▧ **Milestones**: What clear milestones do you want to be reached and by when along the way?

■ **RAG rating**: Where in the data are things going better than expected (colour coded green), as expected (colour coded amber), and worse than expected (colour coded red) at this point in the year.

 (All leaders)   **Implement all support / follow-up procedures**

Securing progress by not letting anyone achieve anything less than their best

For secondary schools, the latest set of data will help identify the students who are eligible for Oxbridge and the Russell Group universities, as well as medicine, veterinary, and dentistry. Applications needing to be sent this month means this is an urgent piece of work for completion. For primary and secondary schools and the rest of the school, with your first round of data in, it is time to get the pupils who aren't making as much progress as they should be back on track. Use the following to ensure the right kind of support is being given to support the pupils most effectively.

Differentiated support to help pupils get back on track:

Short-term support for underachievement in **one subject by a grade**.

Medium-term support for underachievement in **one subject by more than a grade**.

Medium-term support for underachievement in **a number of subjects by a grade**.

Intensive support for underachievement in **a number of subjects by more than a grade**.

Short-term support: Underachievement in one subject by a grade (issue is narrow and shallow)

Those pupils underachieving in one or two subjects by a grade should need little effort and little support to get back on track. Usually, an interview with the pupil, the relevant teacher, and possibly the parents should be enough to ensure the pupil gets back on track with a clear steer of direction in this particular subject. The issue is usually something topic or subject specific that the pupil found particularly challenging.

Medium-term support: Underachievement in one subject by more than a grade (issue is narrow and deep)

Those pupils underachieving in one subject by more than a grade will need some more significant support to get back on track. An interview with the pupil, relevant teachers and the parents will be needed, and a support plan agreed for half a term to ensure the pupil gets back on track with a clear and focused steer in this particular subject. The issue is usually a deep-rooted inability in a particular skill or misunderstanding of a particular key concept in that subject that has a knock-on effect into other areas within the subject. This will need time to correct and embed.

Medium-term support: Underachievement in a number of subjects by a grade (issue is broad and shallow)

Those pupils underachieving in a number of subjects by a grade will also need some significant support to get back on track. An interview with the pupil, relevant teachers, and the parents will be needed, and a support plan agreed for half a term to ensure the pupil gets back on track with a clear and focused steer in these particular subjects. The issue is usually the pupil's ability within a broad skill (reading/writing/numeracy) which affects a number of subjects. Alternatively, there could be issues outside of the classroom that have affected schoolwork. This will also need some time to correct and embed.

Intensive support: Underachievement in a number of subjects by more than a grade (issue is broad and deep)

Those pupils underachieving in a number of subjects by more than a grade will need sustained and determined effort and support to get back on track. An interview with the pupil, relevant teachers, and the parents will be needed, and a support plan agreed for a term to ensure the pupil gets back on track with a clear and focused steer in these particular subjects. There will be a number of issues which will all need addressing. The main danger here is the pupil not having the resilience/self-belief and they give up. Having frequent meetings to help get them back on track will work well in supporting and growing the pupils' self-esteem.

All of the above applies equally to teachers and middle leaders. Where a teacher has a number of pupils (and a head of department who is leading a number of teachers) who are not achieving as much as they should be achieving, organise a minuted meeting with them to discuss the issues and agree subsequent strategies and support to effectively address these issues. Set a review date to monitor progress.

A copy of the individual support plan can be found in September and an electronic copy can be downloaded from the School Leader's Resources page at: www.schoolleaderdevelopment.com.

(All leaders) Implement all quality assurance procedures

Securing progress by others internally or externally checking that what we do is best practice

At this point in the year, the first round of quality assurance checks to see that what we expect to see in place, is in place. This includes checking that the new students (Reception, Year 7, or Year 12) and new staff, including trainee teachers, have settled in. Before taking action and quality assuring your department's or your school's work, consider the following six strategies to help ensure that what you are doing is fit for purpose and effective. Having a different pair of internal eyes at this stage should be sufficient to check (unless there have been issues in the past). Is what we say in our intention being implemented? Here are a number of methods by which we can quality assure the work of the department or the school. Use these to provide evidence that the methods by which leaders lead, teachers teach, and pupils learn is optimal. Where learning, teaching, and leadership are sub-optimal, this needs to be identified, reported, and supported with the sharing of best practice and a plan of action.

Quantitative measures: Data analysis

Analysis of the assessment data is the clearest method of demonstrating impact. Progress over time should show all pupils achieving at or above the expected level of attainment, which is the target. Patterns in the data may emerge of individual pupils and small or large groups of pupils showing variations in that attainment. A question would therefore arise for leaders asking why those patterns are taking place? This may indicate that the transference of understanding, in terms of what to do and how to produce accurate work, may be an issue.

Qualitative measures: Book looks

A great starting place to see progress in knowledge is in pupils' books.

■ *Quality of work in pupils' books:* Looking through the pupils' books there should be clear progress in the increasing accuracy and amount of detail in the work from the start of the book to the most current work.

■ *More challenging language:* The language and breadth of language used is increasingly diverse and more varied through the book. More challenging words are used more accurately and indicate progress in understanding and expression.

- *More complex writing:* The complexity of writing with more compound and complex sentences and increased use of adjectives and adverbs, as pupils think more knowledgeably and skilfully, are indicators of progress in writing with greater understanding.

- *More detailed feedback:* The feedback given to the pupils, through self-assessment, peer assessment, or teacher assessment, and the responses to that feedback, are increasingly detailed, showing a higher degree of knowledge being understood and applied.

Qualitative measures: Book scrutiny

These initial findings in one pupil's book can then be triangulated by looking in a number of pupils' books to see how well the development of the pupils' knowledge has been a focus of the teacher. Looking through the scheme of work and triangulating it with the work in pupils' books over time, it will be possible to identify how the writing is (or is not!) more knowledgeable over time through seeing detailed writing and complexity of language being increasingly developed.

Qualitative measures: Observations

Observations of the lesson will also be able to indicate whether skills, theories, concepts, and knowledge are being explicitly taught by the teacher and learnt by the pupils during the lesson or not. During the lesson, the pupils should be learning increasingly difficult skills, theories, concepts, and knowledge as both the lesson and especially the year progresses. This should correspond with the equivalent place in the scheme of work or programme of study.

Qualitative measures: Learning walks

Learning walks around a department or a school will identify patterns across several classes. Patterns may emerge that require praise and/or follow-up with a particular faculty or group of teachers. During a learning walk, key skills, or knowledge-related issues for leaders to check include ensuring all classes are following the school's expectations, as well as being on track with the department's scheme of work and programme of study.

Qualitative measures: Feedback

There is no more direct way of checking how effective the leadership, teaching, and learning in the school is, than by asking questions directly to those involved. Use any of the strategies below to obtain a rich set of data to inform your report and provide some great quotes from parents, students, and staff.

- Survey (online or on paper) – useful for the breadth of data and to elicit patterns

- Focus group/Working party – useful for gaining informed feedback and constructive criticism

- Interviews (individual or group) – useful for being able to unpack reasons behind issues

- Evaluations – useful in gaining quick feedback to aid future improvements

Qualitative measures: Document scrutiny

Once sufficient evidence has been gathered, a view can be taken as to the quality of the work taking place; this view should be triangulated against **the success criteria/measure of success** communicated by the department/school say in their policies, handbook etc. so there is a clear connection that what it says on the tin (the intention and implementation of education) is in the tin (the experience pupils receive at school). The following documentation should help your quality assurance programme gather the evidence to effectively quality assure the leadership, teaching, and learning being experienced in the school.

INTENTION	IMPLEMENTATION
■ Agreements	■ Audit of work
■ Code of conduct	■ Displays of work
■ Consultations	■ Monitoring and tracking programme
■ Diagrams/posters	■ Learning walk summaries
■ Documentation	■ Logs
■ Handbook	■ Minutes of meetings
■ Induction programme	■ Observation and feedback
■ Information/Advice/Guidance (IAG)	■ Quality assurance (internal)
■ Plans	■ Quality assurance (external)
■ Policies	■ Support programmes
■ Programme of Study	
■ Schedules	
■ Schemes of Work	
■ Statements of intent	

 (Senior leaders)   Confirm admission arrangements

Securing progress by having a clear vision for the future

For secondary schools, the end of October sees confirmation of pupil numbers and the next round of admissions. This is the time when it may be necessary to consult on admission arrangements and ensure that either the school continues to get sufficient pupils through the door or has a clear plan of action for either reduction or expansion.

- **Check**: Ensure that what you are doing is up to date and compliant (see Chapter 15 for useful websites).

- **Consult**: Get as many views as is reasonable from the local community (parents, other schools, the Local Education Authority) to ensure you get a strong understanding of the areas of the strengths and issues that need addressing.

- **Save time**: Get copies/model examples of what you want and amend them to what you need.

- **Propose the best**: Provide a proposal that incorporates research and shares best practice in what you do, e.g. in staff In-Service Education and Training (INSET)/CPD.

- **Propose the most workable solution**: Pilot your proposal with a few trusted colleagues to give you feedback on your proposal. Review and tweak accordingly.

 (All leaders)   Update all plans and CPD

Securing progress by checking we are achieving our targets and implementing improvements.

Updating the FIP, SIP, and SEF is the first formal evaluation of the year, will be the foundation for your report to the SLT or Governors, and will have within it the seeds of the work ahead. Early and swift action to redress any issues is essential.
Before completing the plans and forms, consider the following:

- Have you clearly articulated what you and others need to do, and when and where regarding updating the FIP/SIP/SEF?

- Have you given people involved in the process an opportunity to feedback and give their views as to what they think is going well and what could be improved?

- What is the deadline for the work to be completed?

- What clear milestones are to be reached along the way?

- Have you included updating the statutory areas of Behaviour/Attendance/ SEN (including Education and Health Care Plans – EHCPs)/LAC (Looked After Children)/Behaviour/Attendance/Safeguarding/Careers?

■ Have you cross-checked your actions against the latest inspection criteria and that you are Ofsted ready?

■ What should people do if there is a problem?

■ How and when are you going to follow up with the information that is recorded?

■ What leadership and teaching CPD implications arise from this update?

 (Senior leaders)   Prepare all stakeholder surveys

Securing progress by listening to our stakeholders and delivering an improved service as a result

As the school has now settled into some hopefully good routines, whether primary or secondary, this is a good time to check in with staff, pupils, and parents and take their views as to how well the school is doing to support the wellbeing and work of staff and pupils and the level of communication and support being experienced by parents. To help prepare your surveys, explore what others have written or are doing. Higton (2016) and Jerrim (2019) offer some useful insights and Ofsted on their website give some useful guidance. More information on these can be found in Chapter 15 at the end of this book. Also, use online tools such as Survey Monkey, Google Docs, or Google Sheets to work on key documents or data concurrently with your team and ensure you work as effectively as possible.

Before sending anything out to pupils, parents, and staff, consider the following:

■ Are you clear and have you communicated to relevant staff what needs to happen, and by when and by whom?

■ What are the biggest challenges that lie ahead and how are those challenges going to be addressed?

■ Keep it simple: Include both numeric (quantitative) and text-based (qualitative) questions.

■ Propose the best: Provide a proposal that incorporates research and shares best practice in what you do, e.g. in staff INSET/CPD. See Chapter 15, "Surveys/ Questionnaires", for electronic examples.

■ Save time: Use Google Forms or Survey Monkey to create/re-create examples of what you want and amend to what you need. Incorporate questions that occur in the Ofsted surveys, so you have evidence to hand for your next inspection.

- Keep it flexible: Once your proposal is live, welcome feedback on what is going well and how it could be improved further. Review and tweak accordingly.

- Propose the most workable solution: If you have time, pilot your proposal with a few trusted colleagues to give you feedback on your proposal. This will ensure that your proposal is as successful as it can be.

 (All leaders) Arrange Parents' Evenings

Securing progress by mobilising support at home

Whether primary, or secondary, parents form the third side of the triangle between the school, pupils, and home. Having the parents on board and with you is a significant advantage when working with the young people in our care. Parents' Evenings are the time in the year when that relationship can be significantly developed. This is also a good time to send out the parent questionnaires that have just been created. To help arrange the best Parents' Evenings, explore what others are doing. Online sources, such as SIMS, ParentMail, and Groupcall, give some useful guidance and support. More information on these can be found in Chapter 15 at the end of this book. Also, use online tools such as Google Docs or Google Sheets to work on key documents or data concurrently with your team and ensure you work as effectively as possible.

I have placed Parents' Evenings to begin in January, as there is a term's progress to discuss with parents; however, there is no reason why they cannot start earlier if you wish. See January for more detailed information. However, before embarking on arranging a Parents' Evening, use the following checklist to help you prepare them. An electronic version of the Parents' Evening checklist can be downloaded from the School Leader's Resources page at: www.schooll eaderdevelopment.com.

PARENTS' EVENING CHECKLIST FOR HEADS OF YEAR AND SENIOR LEADERS

Action	Actioned by ... Date by ...
Letters/texts to parents written and sent/PTA/Careers invited	4 weeks before
Letters/booking sheets to pupils written and out	3 weeks before
Remind pupils of upcoming Parents' Evening in tutor time/ assembly	3 weeks before
Assessment data prepared, copied, and ready	2 weeks before
Food and drink for staff on the night booked	2 weeks before
Attendance/punctuality/behaviour/achievement info prepared	2 weeks before
Notes for staff bulletin/briefing communicated	2 weeks before
Ring target pupils to ensure attendance	2 weeks before
Display boards updated	2 weeks before

PARENTS' EVENING CHECKLIST FOR HEADS OF YEAR AND SENIOR LEADERS

Action	Actioned by ...	Date by ...
Outside agencies attending confirmed		2 weeks before
Check noticeboards are tidy and presentable		2 weeks before
Subject/Course Information Sheet (Key Stage 4) prepared if needed		2 weeks before
Information for the website and TV screen communicated		2 weeks before
Outside agencies Education Welfare Officer (EWO/pupil support) contacted and organised		2 weeks before
Reminder texts to parents sent		2 weeks before
Lettings cancelled		2 weeks before
Front of House – staff organised		2 weeks before
Personal Social and Heath Education (PSE) display/citizenship updated		2 weeks before
Rooming organised/hall booked		2 weeks before
Books marked and information for parents prepared and ready		2 weeks before
Organise Seniors (Head of Sixth) or Prefects (Head of Year) to help		2 weeks before
Booking sheet distributed to pupils		2 weeks before
Remind pupils of upcoming Parents' Evening every couple of days		2 weeks before
Uniform information ready		I week before
All staff have ID cards		I week before
Electronic equipment booked		I week before
Any info regarding payments organised		I week before
Reminder texts to parents sent		I week before
Cleaning arrangement before and after the evening booked		I week before
Staff car parking and signs sorted		I week before
Name cards and up-to-date staff list ready		I week before
Flowers for reception and tablecloths ordered		I week before
See Site Team regarding security for the evening		I week before
Front of House – pupils involved agreed and ready		I week before
Remind pupils of upcoming Parents' Evening in tutor time/assembly		I week before
Public areas check all tidy and clean		The day
Reminder texts to parents sent		The day
Sign-in registers, staff locators, and information for parents out		The evening
Absent Staff notice displayed		The evening
Hall and rooms cleared away afterwards		The evening
SLT in attendance		The evening
Notification for meeting slots and evening beginning/end done		The evening
Water for staff/refreshments for parents available		The evening
Notice for entrance displayed		The evening
Organise Seniors (Head of Sixth) or Prefects (Head of Year) to help out		The evening
Thankyou cards/email out		Day after
Tidy check		Day after

🕐 **(Senior leaders)   Arrange successful transition programmes**

Securing progress by having clear, ambitious goals for our pupils

---

With Year 6, Year 11, and Year 13 experiencing that stage of education for the last time, attention must be turned to ensuring the school is clear about the processes and procedures the pupils need to follow to successfully transition to the next stage of their education and to ensure that potential new Year 7's and potential new sixth formers have a clear recruitment process.

Being in the top year can be enjoyable whilst there is a perception that you will always be the biggest fish in the pool. Preparing pupils for leaving is the first glimpse that may destabilise that dream and bring a dose of reality to the pupils leaving, helping them begin to realise that there are larger ponds in which to swim on the horizon and that it is only a matter of time before they move from the comfortable, confident, and known, to the uncertain, more challenging unknown.

To help prepare the best transition programme, explore what others have written or are doing. The Department for Education (DfE) offers some useful insights and companies such as SIMS and Education Advisers on their websites give some useful guidance as to pupil recruitment and destinations. More information on these can be found in Chapter 15 at the end of this book. Also, use online tools such as Google Docs or Google Sheets to work on key documents or data concurrently with your team and ensure you work as effectively as possible.

Here are some points to help ensure the pupils go on to the best and most appropriate destination of choice:

- **Aim for the best**: Use assembly time to bring in ex-pupils or aspirational speakers to ensure that pupils aim high and do not go for the easiest or nearest option first. Mobilise a co-ordinator to manage applications for Oxbridge, Russell Group universities, and their equivalents ahead of the October deadline.

- **Build in safety nets**: Ensure in the pupils' choices that there are some safe options that can be mobilised if things do not work out quite as planned.

- **Consult**: Get the pupils to gather as many views as possible about their road ahead. This will help develop their independent learning skills and will help provide them with more of a richness and breadth of choice than would otherwise be the case.

- **Save time**: Get copies /model examples of what you want to provide and amend them to what you need.

■ **Bring in experts**: Bring in ex-pupils, newly qualified teachers (NQTs), parents etc. to talk about what they have experienced and allow other voices than the "school" to talk to the pupils.

■ **Plan**: Have a clear plan in place that takes them (almost literally) from here to there, or there to here.

Moments that count throughout the year:

You never know when the investment of time and care will be repaid with interest!

Some years ago, a family moving from Scotland to the South East were awarded a place at our single-sex boys' school. The parent was emphatic that her twin boys needed the influence of girls and a mixed-sex education. After weeks of appeals and complaints to the Local Education Authority, the parent was surprised to receive a telephone call from me with an invitation to come in for a chat about supporting and possibly resolving her issue.

I took her for a quick stroll around school on a normal Wednesday morning as we chatted. She was astonished by the air of quiet study in most classrooms, the exuberance of the boys on the playing field, and enthusiasm on obvious display in a language classroom as boys vied to answer questions in French. At the end of the tour, having offered to write to the LEA, she surprised me by asking if her boys could come in the following day.

The twins joined our school and flourished in all areas of the curriculum, music, and sport. Three years later and a visit by Ofsted, the same parent was the first on the phone asking to speak to our Ofsted inspectors. I was delighted and she clearly convinced them that our provision not only met her sons' needs, but was excellent in every way.

You never know which are the conversations which will tell, so make them all count.

Paul Ramsey, Headteacher

 (Senior leaders)   Prepare consultation on next year

Securing progress through investigating the most efficient and effective method of education

---

Once the trajectory of the year ahead is a little clearer as regards pupil numbers, the great task of aligning pupil numbers, finances, the curriculum, classes, and staffing for the year ahead begins. To help prepare the best integrated framework, explore what others have written or are doing. Slater (2009), Reynolds (2014), and

Solomon (2016) offer some useful insights and the DfE on their website gives some useful guidance. More information on these can be found in Chapter 15 at the end of this book. Also, use online tools such as Google Docs or Google Sheets to work on key documents or data concurrently with your team and ensure you work as effectively as possible.

The following considerations need to be taken into account:

PUPIL NUMBERS	FINANCES	CURRICULUM	CLASSES	STAFFING
Minimum and maximum numbers of pupils in each year group + In-year admissions	Minimum and maximum income generated as a result	Incorporate statutory curriculum requirements and recent changes	Minimum and maximum class sizes to deliver the curriculum	Staffing requirements to deliver this

Ahead of any large meetings/communications that are distributed regarding the key work of the school and future plans, consider the following to help inform your work:

- Are you clear and have you communicated to relevant staff what needs to happen, and by when and by whom?

- What are the biggest challenges that lie ahead and how are those challenges going to be addressed?

- Save time: Get copies/model examples of what you want and amend them to what you need.

- Keep information evidence based.

- Propose the best: Provide a proposal that incorporates research and shares best practice in what you do, e.g. in staff INSET/CPD.

- Keep it flexible: Once your proposal is live, welcome feedback on what is going well and how it could be improved further. Review and tweak accordingly.

Summary and checklist for October

LEADER ACTION	FOCUS	SENIOR LEADERS	MIDDLE LEADERS
Evaluate and celebrate	Open Evening and Open Week		
Action	Complete and return the autumn term census		
	Set up a scheme of work (SOW) for Autumn 2	▨	
	Implement autumn monitoring and tracking		
	Implement Monitoring and Tracking programme 1		
	Implement Coursework, Catch Up, and Revision programmes		
	Quality assurance – Autumn programme starts		
	Confirm admission arrangements		▨
	SIP/FIP/SEF/ and CPD updated		▨
Arrange	Parent/pupil/staff surveys		▨
	Parents' Evenings		
	Pupil recruitment		▨
	Integrated Framework		▨

November

November is the month to keep focused and be resilient. It is a time where significant gains can be made, or lost, as everyone and everything is tested to the full.

November needs to be experienced with determination and tenacity.

DOI: 10.4324/9781003129691-4

Introduction: November

November provides the response to the emerging data from October. As well as implementing the lift or drive that is needed to get slower pupils/staff up to speed, it is also the month of preparation – for the end of term and larger scale projects to be completed in the year ahead. Here is what you have ahead of you in November.

NOVEMBER SUMMARY		
KEY		
👍 Action that evaluates & celebrates previous work	⟫ Action that supports current work	⟲ Action that prepares future work
Statutory activity (higher priority)		**Non-statutory activity (lower priority)**
Action	*Leaders*	*School focus for November*
⟲	Middle leaders	Prepare end of term tests
⟲	Senior leaders	Agree end of autumn /start of spring term arrangements
⟲	All leaders	Prepare options process (KS4/5)
⟲	Senior leaders	Prepare capital bids
⟫	All leaders	Update staff recruitment for spring term
⟫	All leaders	Update Coursework, Catch Up, and Revision programmes
⟫	Senior leaders	Carry out surveys with parents/staff and pupils
⟫	All leaders	Pupil destinations/recruitment process underway
⟫	Senior leaders	End of term tests all completed

As November starts, create an opportunity at your next leadership team/ department meeting to discuss the following standing agenda items:

- **Staffing and safeguarding**: Are there any staffing and/or safeguarding concerns to be urgently addressed this month, especially with the October 31st resignation deadline looming?

- **Calendar**: Are there any pinch points this month which need to be carefully managed beforehand?

- **Trips and school activities**: Are there any trips or large group activities this month which need to be carefully managed?

- **Website and communications**: Is the website up to date and are parents/pupils/ staff clear about what is happening this month? Is there robust, challenging, and engaging online work available for pupils to complete if needed?

- **Inspection ready**: Which areas need addressing this month to ensure we are on track with our work?

The rationale for the other actions taking place this month, and in this order, include that an action is *more important* or needs doing *more urgently*, has a higher priority and therefore comes earlier in the month and vice versa. An action may be *part of a process* and so must happen before one action, but after another. Also, certain actions are *fixed* to events outside of the school's control and so these actions are tied to a particular date in the calendar (for example, external exams) or are actions *related to a fixed* event.

With November underway, we have plenty of time to arrange the end of term tests which then ties into a wider discussion and round of decisions related to the end of the autumn term and the start of spring term arrangements. Having completed a broad review of the curriculum, earlier in the term, another large piece of work is to update and put out to consultation the options process. As the wheels of education continue to move forwards, November also sees the government loosening the purse strings and allowing schools to bid for significant funds for school improvement.

As the deadline of 31st October for resignations has now passed, it is necessary to put out advertisements for any staffing needed in January. Following on from the latest round of tests and coursework completion, it is important that the coursework, catch up, and revision programme tracker is updated, and improvements are starting to be seen. While all this is happening, staff, parents, and pupils can be consulted as to how well they view the progress of the school. This helps inform the way in which the school recruits and retains pupils. With the end of November comes those end of term assessments, late enough to show learning, but early enough to be marked before the end of term. Here are November's actions in a little more detail.

(Middle leaders) Arrange end of term tests

Securing progress through arranging an assessment of what has been learnt so far

For both primary and secondary schools, in arranging the end of term tests, it should be clear from the programme of study and scheme of work what learning needs to be tested. To help prepare the best assessments, explore what others have written or are doing. Kyriakides (2008), Paterson (2013), Coe (2014), and Christodoulou (2016) offer some useful insights and a number of groups, including PiXL and the Department for Education (DfE), on their websites, give some useful guidance. More information on these can be found in Chapter 15 at the end of this book. Also, use online tools such as Google Docs or Google Sheets to work on key documents or data concurrently with your team and ensure you work as effectively as possible. Before you start the process of arranging the end of term tests, use the following to ensure the process is as effective as it can be.

Assessment preparation for teachers

In preparing pupils for their end of term assessments, here are ten effective strategies that provide good value for money for teachers to ensure their pupils are assessment ready.

- Peer quizzes: Pupils quiz each other on what has been learnt so far and mark/grade each other.

- Pupils revise and teacher tests previously learnt and current work, using online programmes such as Quizlet.

- Have pupils explain why an answer is right *and* why an answer is wrong.

- Use flash cards to focus pupils' minds on key terms and concepts, using online resources such as Kahoot.

- Develop exam stamina by training pupils to revise in short, intensive sessions and answer questions over longer periods of time.

- Use past papers to develop pupil exam vocabulary.

- Have pupils use Mind Maps to organise complex/detailed projects.

- Have pupils use Literacy Maps to encapsulate key terms and concepts.

- Use Spaced Retrieval in schemes of work to keep previously learnt work fresh in pupils' minds.

- Do not accept classwork or homework that is below expectation from pupils. Have them re-draft and re-submit.

Assessment preparation for leaders

In arranging the end of term assessments, confirm the process of assessment with school leaders and the exams officer and publicise.

Use the following to help prepare your mock exams in November for Key Stage 4 and in January for Key Stage 5:

- Ensure all pupils have target grades given to them for each subject.

- Ensure all pupils and parents know those target grades.

- Ensure all books/files have a completed tracker sheet that records test results throughout the year.

- Confirm arrangements for mock examinations, a mock exam revision programme, and study leave.

- Confirm arrangements for end of term test marking, reporting, and data input schedule.

- Consistently prepare staff and pupils for the tests, consulting and communicating agreed expectations.

- Present the process to the Senior Leadership Team (SLT) and heads of department, so everyone is clear on the process and key deadlines.

- Discuss with the SLT/Governors as to how the process is to be quality assured and how to ensure that the information being presented is accurate and that staff are consistent in how the assessments are being carried out and data recorded.

- Set up a Question/Analysis spreadsheet and discuss results at the next department meeting.

- Set up a whole school data analysis spreadsheet and discuss results at the next SLT meeting.

 (Senior leaders)   **Prepare end and start of term arrangements**

Securing progress through a continued focus on teaching, learning, and making good progress

---

We are here already?! The end of term can be a time, especially at the end of the autumn term, when teaching and learning can become frayed and unfocused and as a result, leadership is responsive to events rather than directing and leading them. To help prepare a calm and well-organised end of term/start of term, explore what others have written or are doing. The DfE (2020b) offer some useful insights and the DfE and The Key on their websites give some useful guidance. More information on these can be found in Chapter 15 at the end of this book. Also, use online tools such as Google Docs or Google Sheets to work on key documents or data concurrently with your team and ensure you work as effectively as possible. Use the following ahead of any communications to help inform the end of term/ start of term arrangements to help keep the end and start of term focused and positive.

- Have "End of Term/Start of Term" and "Emergency school closure procedures" as agenda items and get as many views as is reasonable to ensure you get a strong understanding of what needs to be done to wrap up the term, specify any work to be done over the Christmas break, and start the next term.

- Save time: Use last year's information/guidance that went out and amend to what you need.

- Co-ordinate: Check what other schools are doing and, if applicable, align your holidays with theirs.

- Propose the best: Provide a proposal that incorporates research and shares best practice in what you do, e.g. in staff In-Service Education and Training (INSET)/continuing professional development (CPD).

- Propose the most workable solution: Ensure to include end of term celebrations such as Christmas lunches, staff Christmas party, the carol concert, etc. as well as expectations for end of term lessons. Pilot your proposal with a few trusted colleagues to give you feedback on your proposal. This will ensure that your proposal is as successful as it can be.

- Keep it flexible: Once your proposal is live, welcome feedback on what is going well and how it could be improved further. Review and tweak accordingly. Put out the final version when ready.

 (All leaders)   Arrange Options process (KS4/5)
Ensuring the best curriculum choices for the pupils are made by the pupils

Following discussions from the integrated framework, the curriculum proposals available to put to pupils should be clearer. For secondary schools, ahead of that process beginning, and to help prepare the best options process for your pupils, explore what others have written or are doing. The DfE and Ofqual offer some useful insights and their websites give some useful guidance. More information on these can be found in Chapter 15 at the end of this book. Also, use online tools such as Google Docs or Google Sheets to work on key documents or data concurrently with your team and ensure you work as effectively as possible. Use the following to help ensure that the process is as effective as possible.

To help check that everything that needs to be done has been considered, use the following chart to help confirm it has. An electronic copy of this options process checklist can be found and downloaded from the School Leader's Resources page at: www.schoolleaderdevelopment.com.

TASKS	JANUARY	FEBRUARY	MARCH
Review labour market information (LMI) to inform options			
Carry out options survey/curriculum audit to scope courses			
Review and agree the curriculum offer			
Outline curriculum and options process to stakeholders			
Carry out consultation of curriculum offer			
Consult pupil groups in registration			
Confirm options offer with leadership team			
Confirm options offer with Governors			
Update website with subject information			
Clarify options process at staff INSET			
Arrange Heads of Faculty to present subjects			
Distribute Options Booklet for review and amending			
Distribute final Options Booklet			
Arrange/communicate Options guidance			
Options Booklet return deadline			
Communicate Options guidance at Parents' evening			
Arrange Options Evening and distribute options form			
Arrange and communicate Parent/Pupil Options surgeries			
Option forms returned from ...			
Option forms returned – final deadline ...			
Collate the list in Excel			
See pupils needing changes			
Communicate final options list			

Moments that count in November: Options

In the music room one break time between classes, a Year 10 pupil came in and introduced himself. He pointed out that he had made a mistake with his options and would it be possible to change to Music instead of their current chosen subject? "Not really" I said, "the options process is meant to be a considered and thorough process. Pupils should have given lots of thought to what they were choosing to do; therefore changing options at this stage is not really possible". Maintaining persistence, he asked if he could learn to play the piano.

"Not a problem. What do you want to learn?"
"The piano".
"Any particular piece?"
"Yes. I'd like to play Beethoven's Moonlight Sonata".
"That's about Grade 5 standard and way too hard for a beginner on Grade 1. Which part?"
"The first movement".
"OK".

We arranged the first lesson and within two weeks, he had learnt to play the first movement of Beethoven's Moonlight Sonata from memory. Clearly, here was a pupil who had a musical talent and some potential. We had a discussion with the senior leadership team and arranged for him to change options. A good move. He went on to achieve an A* and continued to A level and to study Music for a degree. All of this from a pupil whose first language wasn't English and who was the first in his family to go to university.

A couple of years later, an invitation arrived in the post. It was an invitation to his graduation performance with the following message "Please come and see how your work finished up. If it wasn't for you, I wouldn't be where I am today and receiving a degree".

Whilst schools are increasingly under pressure to deliver a narrower curriculum, this can at times be counter-productive. There is space, and a need, to create moments that count for pupils, in helping them find their talent, find their place in society, and help them realise their unique potential.

 (Senior leaders)   **Arrange capital bids**

Securing progress through improving the learning environment

This is the time of year when the government opens up funding availability to schools. Bidding for significant amounts of additional money is where much progress can be made in terms of improving the facilities and the working environment of a school. From new windows to a new sports hall, or extension, this is the once-a-year opportunity to make a dream come true. To help prepare the best bids, explore what others have written or are doing – especially primary schools who may wish to submit a joint bid. The IDfE and other groups such as Grantsonline or Grants4schools offer some useful insights and on their websites give some useful guidance. More information on these can be found in Chapter 15 at the end of this book. Also, use online tools such as Google Docs or Google Sheets to work on key documents or data concurrently with your team and ensure you work as effectively as possible. Before starting the process, consider the following:

▓ If there isn't a strategic three-to-five-year plan, consult: Get as many views as is reasonable (10% minimum) to ensure you get a strong understanding of what the school's building needs are.

▓ Save time: Get a professional on board who has secured significant bids before. Spending £25,000 to secure £1m of funding is money well spent.

▓ Propose the best: The pupils deserve the best. Provide a proposal that incorporates research and shares best practice in what you do, e.g. in staff INSET/CPD.

▓ Propose the most workable solution: Pilot your proposal with a few trusted colleagues to give you feedback on your proposal. This will ensure that your proposal is as successful as it can be.

▓ Keep it flexible: Once your proposal is live, welcome feedback on what is going well and how it could be improved further. Review and tweak accordingly.

 (All leaders)   **Update staff recruitment for spring term**

Securing progress by ensuring continuous, high-quality teaching and learning

---

With the October 31st deadline having now passed for both primary and secondary school leaders, it will be clear as to the permanent staffing that will be in place in January. Any changes to this need to be filled as soon as possible to avoid the need for supply or job sharing in the new term. Use the following to support your work in replacing much-needed staff:

▓ Confirm resignations with effect from 31st December.

▓ Consult and liaise with relevant staff over any deletions/amendments to existing/creation of new roles.

▓ Amend job descriptions as required.

- Identify and liaise with any internal candidates that may be suitable for the new role.

- Advertise the new role.

- Interview and secure staffing for all roles in January.

- What is the deadline for the staffing to be completed?

- What clear milestones are to be reached along the way?

- What should people do if there is a problem?

This can be very time-consuming. Also use January's checklist to keep this important work manageable.

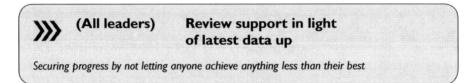

》》》 (All leaders)   Review support in light of latest data up

Securing progress by not letting anyone achieve anything less than their best

With the first round of whole school or department data coming through from the first set of marks from half term tests, comes an opportunity to celebrate and an opportunity to learn. Results that are at, above, and beyond what you are expecting means the learning process, outlined below, is working very well and is a moment to celebrate and evaluate why that is – what great leadership, teaching, and learning are going on that can be shared?

However, results that are not what you are expecting means the learning process is not working as well as it could be and present an opportunity to carry out a gap analysis and urgently correct the trajectory of progress. The issue may be related to the leadership, the teaching, or the learning within the learning process. The table below illustrates some examples of this.

ISSUE	CHECK			
Inconsistent results between classes	Scheme of work	Programme of study	Assessment process	Quality of teaching
Inconsistent results for a pupil group	Prior attainment (High/Middle/Low)	Target grades (High/Middle/Low)	Groups (Special Educational Needs – SEN/pupil premium –PP/English as an Additional Language – EAL)	Gender (boys/girls)
Inconsistent results for a teacher	Pitch (Difficulty)	Pace (Adaptability)	Differentiation (Accessibility)	Engagement (Style)

If from the data there are inconsistent results between teachers, consider the Education Endowment Foundation (EEF)'s guidance (2018) to see if the school needs to make improvements to the teaching and learning experience.

EDUCATION ENDOWMENT FOUNDATION'S TOP 10 RECOMMENDED SUPPORT STRATEGIES TO IMPROVE PROGRESS

Strategy	Cost	Strength of Evidence	Impact (months)
Feedback	£	✓✓✓	+8
Metacognition and self-regulation	£	✓✓✓✓	+7
Reading comprehension strategies	£	✓✓✓✓	+6
Collaborative learning	£	✓✓✓✓	+5
Oral language interventions	£	✓✓✓✓	+5
Peer tutoring	£	✓✓✓✓	+5
Mastery learning	£	✓✓✓	+5
Homework (secondary)	£	✓✓	+5
One to one tuition	££££	✓✓✓✓	+5
Phonics	£	✓✓✓✓✓	+4

When you have identified any strategies that are likely to improve school-wide practice, the next step is to look at the data for inconsistent results, or consistently poor results between pupils and any more specific patterns across the department/school.

> Are there patterns in a particular group of pupils not achieving to the expected level?
>
> Meet with colleagues to discuss and agree sharing best practice through CPD and pupil intervention.
>
> Staff INSET (e.g. guidance provided at staff meeting/activities during INSET) needs to be put in place to help the team raise the quality or implement a more effective pace to teaching and learning.

If the issue is pupil related, consider the following:

ISSUE	SOLUTION	METHOD
Absence from lessons	Complete the missed work after school	Online work/Catch up programme
Inability to answer questions	Revision/exam practice/ targeted intervention	Revision groups/practice tests/ study-buddy
Insufficient work completed	Opportunities to catch up	Catch up programme/1-to-1 support/small group work

Having a strong programme of general support available to them ensures that pupils do not slip too far behind and continue to make sufficient progress.

Last but not least, when you have identified any strategies that are likely to improve progress for key groups of pupils, the next step is to look at the inconsistent results of an individual teacher.

> For each individual teacher, are there patterns in a particular group of pupils not achieving to the expected level?
>
> Meet with colleagues to discuss and agree any necessary staff training and pupil intervention.
>
> Focused CPD (e.g. peer observation, team teaching, or specific training) needs to be put in place to help the team raise the quality or implement a more effective pace to teaching and learning.

For those pupils and staff underachieving for the first time, implement the actions as suggested in October. For those pupils and staff who are continuing to underachieve, implement an individual support plan as suggested in September.

> **》》》** **(Senior leaders) – Carry out all stakeholder surveys**
>
> *Securing progress through a better understanding of how learning could be more effectively done*

Hopefully, you have created your surveys using Google Docs or Survey Monkey and can email out the surveys. Emailing to pupils and staff is straightforward; however, this method also requires schools to have parent email addresses up to date, a job that is necessary, but a little like painting the Forth Bridge!

Sending these out to different groups of pupils, parents, and staff each term enables you to have a clear picture as to what is working well at the school, and what needs improving.

> **Sending a survey out each term with a different group of pupils, parents, and staff, but in the same department or year group, can effectively measure progress in how well things are being addressed.**

Use the following questions to help run a well-managed and well-considered process:

- Have you clearly articulated what you and others need to do, and when and where regarding the completion of the questionnaires?

- Have you clearly articulated how staff/pupils' work will benefit as a result of what you are asking people to do?

- What is the deadline for the questionnaires to be completed?

- What should people do if there is a problem?

A turn-around of two weeks with follow-up reminders along the way will be enough to gather the information you need. For it to be significant – as a rule of thumb, annually, you need about 10% of the school's pupil/staff/parent population; thus, at least 4% return each term should be sufficient.

(All leaders)   Pupil destinations/recruitment process starts

Securing progress by clarifying the success and growth of the school

So that your school leavers have a clear goal to aim for, providing far more meaning to the school experience as a result, use the following to help ensure that the department's or the school's leavers' programme is as effective as it could be:

■ Year 13 preparation for interviews at Oxbridge, Russell Group universities and their equivalent should be well underway.

■ Year 11 applications and preparation for interviews at sixth form colleges should also be well underway.

■ Have you clearly articulated what you and others need to do, and when and where regarding induction?

■ Have you clearly articulated how staff/pupils' work will benefit as a result of what you are asking people to do?

■ What is the deadline for the work to be completed?

■ What clear milestones are to be reached along the way?

■ If this is additional to people's work, what should they do about covering their other work that is being missed?

■ What should people do if there is a problem?

 (Senior leaders) End of term tests all completed

Securing progress through recognising and reporting pupil progress in their assessments

To ensure every pupil is included and receives the results from their end of term tests, use the following to check the process you have in place is robust and comprehensive.

■ All pupils have received their latest grades.

■ All parents have received an update and been given their child's latest grades.

■ All books/files/tracker sheets/pupil records have been updated.

■ A question analysis is underway by departments and is put on the agenda for the next department meeting.

- Whole school data analysis is underway by the SLT and is put on the agenda for the next SLT meeting.

- SLT are following up to ensure all tests have been completed and all results have been recorded.

- SLT/Governors are quality assuring that the information being presented is accurate and ensuring that staff are consistent in how the assessments are being carried out and data recorded.

Summary and checklist for November

LEADER ACTION	FOCUS	SENIOR LEADERS	MIDDLE LEADERS
Arrange	End of term tests		
	End of autumn term/start of spring term arrangements		
	Options process (KS4/5)		
	Capital bids		
Action	Update staff recruitment for spring term		
	Update Coursework, Catch Up, and Revision programmes		
	Carry out surveys/questionnaires		
	Pupil destinations/recruitment process underway		
	End of term tests all completed		

December

You've made it! The first and longest term comes to a close.

December is a month of drawing the first major threads together that provide a clear overview of the successes of the autumn term and the challenges that lie ahead.

December is a month to be experienced with joy and celebration.

DOI: 10.4324/9781003129691-5

Introduction: December

December sees the first of three frenetic ends of term as the ongoing work of the school runs out of conveyor belt ahead of the impending holidays. In a rush to get things completed, as well as to enjoy and celebrate the term's achievements, it may be easy for school leaders to be distracted from essential work. The following strategies are for both senior and middle leaders to use at either the whole school or the department level. Here is what you have ahead of you in December.

DECEMBER SUMMARY		
KEY		
👍 Action that evaluates and celebrates previous work	⫸ Action that supports current work	🕐 Action that prepares future work
Statutory activity (higher priority)		Non-statutory activity (lower priority)
Action	Leaders	School focus for December
👍	All leaders	Evaluate results from tests and record/write reports
👍	Senior leaders	Evaluate results from parent, staff, and pupil surveys
⫸	Middle leaders	Update and dust down Schemes of Work for Spring 1
⫸	Senior leaders	Implement Integrated Framework
⫸	All leaders	Update Coursework, Catch Up, and Revision programmes
⫸	All leaders	Update school's evaluation form (SEF)/School Improvement Plan (SIP)/Faculty Improvement Plan (FIP), and continuing professional development (CPD) in light of data
⫸	Senior leaders	Send off Capital bids
⫸	All leaders	Celebrate a term (well) done

As December starts, create an opportunity at your next leadership team/ department meeting to discuss the following standing agenda items:

- **Staffing and safeguarding**: Are there any staffing and/or safeguarding concerns to be urgently addressed this month? How is everyone feeling? Do any changes need to be made to help get everyone through?

- **Calendar**: Are there any pinch points this month which need to be carefully managed beforehand? Applying to December the Key Stage 4 mock exams preparation from November to the Key Stage 5 mock examinations in January will secure an orderly and organised start to the new term.

- **Trips and school activities**: Are there any trips or large group activities this month which need to be carefully managed?

- **Website and communications**: Is the website up to date and are parents/pupils/ staff clear about what is happening this month? Is there robust, challenging, and engaging online work available for pupils to complete if needed?

- **Inspection ready**: Which areas need addressing this month to ensure we are on track with our work?

The rationale for the other actions taking place this month, and in this order, include that an action is *more important* or needs doing *more urgently*, has a higher priority and therefore comes earlier in the month and vice versa. An action may be *part of a process* and so must happen before one action, but after another. Also, certain actions are *fixed* to events outside of the school's control and so these actions are tied to a particular date in the calendar (for example, external exams), or are actions *related to a fixed* event.

A celebration and evaluation of the end of term tests must take place in early December after the tests have been completed but before the school finishes for the holidays. Having previously sent out the surveys to parents, pupils, and staff, this is also the time to gather that information and evaluate its content ahead of the holiday period. Looking ahead, the spring term's schemes of work need to be checked over and prepared, taking into consideration the end of term test results and the feedback from questionnaires.

Having got November wrapped up and preparations for the end of term and January underway, the necessary work for December can begin. Thus, the first attempts at an integrated framework, aiming to bring harmoniously together the tectonic plates of pupil numbers, the curriculum, classes, staffing, and the budget can begin. This is also the time to update the coursework and catch up programme in light of the results and feedback, as well as update the school's evaluation form and school and faculty improvement plans. With Capital bids now put together, it is also time to send these off.

With as much as can be updated and put to bed, the last thing to do is to celebrate the end of term with concerts, festive lunches, and lots of seasonal cheer; finally seeing everyone off the premises and able to close the office door on one more completed autumn term. Here are December's activities in a little more detail.

 (All leaders)   Celebrate end of term assessment results

Securing progress by recognising, publicising, and promoting pupil progress

---

Similar to the October deadline for applications to Oxbridge, the deadline for university courses is on the horizon in January, and so for Sixth Form students, these test results will form the basis of any decisions being made. Also, just before the end of term, take a moment to consider the journey your pupils are making with you so far this year, where they have come from and where they are going to. After writing your report on what the data says, use the following questions to check that you have covered these key points.

Analyse

- Have you recorded and reported your data clearly and succinctly?

- What patterns have emerged related to learning and learners, teaching and teachers, and leadership and leaders?

- How does this data compare to similar data from previous years, and the latest local and national benchmarks?

- What positive and less than positive messages about learning, teaching, and leadership come out of the end of term tests of this year's pupils?

Evaluate

- What targets/goals were set to be achieved in relation to the attainment and progress of this year's pupils and have these targets/goals been achieved, partially achieved, or not achieved?

- What went well and what could have been improved? Have you consulted with key staff involved in the process and enabled them to give their views in relation to this term's end of term tests?

- What do you understand to be the reasons behind any successes and any areas that were less successful in relation to the results and the reporting of those results?

Action

- What follow-up actions need to be made/key messages need to be communicated as a result of your analysis/evaluation, especially in relation to the Key Stage 5 university applications and mock exams in January?

Celebrate

- Before ending the autumn term, this is (hopefully) an important milestone in each pupil's education to date. Use the following to check you have covered all the relevant bases before you send out your report on the end of term tests to the school community.

- Reinforce aspiration. In the end of term assemblies and communications to the school community, celebrate those pupils who have achieved at or above expectations.

 (Senior leaders)   Results from surveys/questionnaires

Securing progress through understanding how learning is and could be more effectively done

---

To help cross-reference how successful the school has been over the year and add context to your survey findings, Lenon (2017), Higton (2017), and Jerrim (2019) offer some useful insights and Ofsted on their website gives some useful guidance. More information on these can be found in Chapter 15 at the end of this book. In addition, using online tools such as Google Forms enables you to efficiently evaluate your work, saving you precious time. Again, before the end of term, take a moment to consider the views of your key stakeholders. After writing your report, use the following questions to check that you have covered these key points.

Analyse

- Have you reported your data clearly and succinctly?

- What patterns have emerged related to learning and learners, teaching and teachers, leadership and leaders, parent communication and support?

- How does this data compare to similar data from previous years, and the latest local and national benchmarks?

- What positive and less than positive messages about learning, teaching, and leadership come out of the end of term tests of this year's pupils?

Evaluate

■ What targets/goals were set to be achieved in relation to pupil, staff, and parent questionnaires and have these targets/goals been achieved, partially achieved, or not achieved?

■ What went well and what could have been improved? Have you consulted with key staff involved in the process and enabled them to give their views?

■ What do you understand to be the reasons behind any successes and any areas that were less successful in relation to both the surveys and the results from those surveys?

Action

■ What follow-up actions need to be made/key messages need to be communicated as a result of your analysis/evaluation?

Celebrate

■ Arrange a method of communicating the positive messages from the questionnaires and celebrate your school's success at an assembly or staff meeting, or by publishing social media posts, or an article for the school's newsletter/website.

■ Create an opportunity to celebrate your school/department's success and make explicit the progress you are making as a school/department.

■ Write letters of appreciation to key teachers and leaders for their notable positive contribution.

■ Wall space and your website are free! Display key positive messages from the questionnaires, as this is a free way to keep reinforcing the message that your school is successful. Therefore, ensure the wall space in your school is used to full effect and display the key results from these questionnaires.

■ Using quotes from the questionnaire on letters and on presentation PowerPoints also helps reinforce the message that your school/department is a success.

 (Middle leaders)   Update Schemes of Work for Spring 1

Securing progress by providing a comprehensive, clear, and achievable curriculum

As you review/prepare your scheme of work for the spring term, use the following to check it is as good as it can be:

- Are the **aims** of the scheme of work and each lesson **realistically high, clearly articulated**, and **ordered coherently** so progress over the scheme of work is **explicit**?

- Is the work to be completed **manageable, challenging**, and **consistently focused on pupil learning**?

- Is there explicit **progression in understanding** from description and facts to analysis and reasoning?

- Is there a clear **increase in the challenge/complexity of knowledge and skills** being learnt?

- Is the work expected to be completed **increasingly longer and harder**?

- Are activities progressing **from the class/group** to the **individual** over time and do they **include homework**?

- Is the **assessment for learning built into each lesson** and does it move **from informal to formal assessment**?

- What **provisions are in place** should anyone fall behind, or finish sooner than expected?

 (Senior leaders) Begin consultation on next year

Securing progress through identifying the most efficient and effective way to work as a school.

Now the trajectory of the year ahead is clearer as regards pupil numbers, the great task of aligning pupil numbers, finances, the curriculum, classes, and staffing for the year ahead begins. The following decisions should have been made and be informing your work this month:

PUPIL NUMBERS	FINANCES	CURRICULUM	CLASSES	STAFFING
Minimum and maximum numbers of pupils in each year group + In-year admissions	Minimum and maximum income generated as a result	Incorporate statutory curriculum requirements and recent changes	Minimum and maximum class sizes to deliver the curriculum	Staffing requirements to deliver this

Ahead of any large meetings/communications that are distributed regarding the key work of the school and future plans, consider the following to help inform your work:

- Have you clearly articulated what you and others need to do, and when and where regarding pupil recruitment, finances, the curriculum, class sizes, and staffing?

- Have you clearly articulated how the work of the school will benefit as a result of what you are asking people to do?

- What is the deadline for each of the pieces of work to be completed?

- What clear milestones are to be reached along the way?

- When will the seperate pieces of work be brought together to review the holistic progress being made?

- If this is additional to people's work, what should they do about covering their other work that is being missed?

- What should people do if there is a problem?

 (All leaders)   Review support in light of latest data

Securing progress by not letting anyone achieve anything less than their best

With the latest round of whole school or department data coming through from the latest assessments comes an opportunity to celebrate and an opportunity to learn. Results that are at, above, and beyond what you are expecting means the learning process, outlined below, is working very well and present a moment to celebrate and evaluate why that is – what great leadership, teaching, and learning are going on that can be shared?

However, results that are not what you are expecting means the learning process is not working as well as it could be and is an opportunity to carry out a gap analysis and urgently correct the trajectory of progress. The issue may be related to the leadership, the teaching, or the learning within the learning process. The table below illustrates some examples of this.

ISSUE	CHECK			
Inconsistent results between classes	Scheme of work	Programme of study	Assessment process	Quality of teaching
Inconsistent results for a pupil group	Prior attainment (High/Middle/Low)	Target grades (High/Middle/Low)	Groups (special educational needs – SEN/pupil premium – PP/ English as an Additional Language – EAL)	Gender (boys/girls)
Inconsistent results for a teacher	Pitch (Difficulty)	Pace (Adaptability)	Differentiation (Accessibility)	Engagement (Style)

If from the data there are inconsistent results between teachers, consider the Education Endowment Foundation (EEF)'s guidance (2018) to see if the school needs to make improvements to the teaching and learning experience.

EDUCATION ENDOWMENT FOUNDATION'S TOP 10 RECOMMENDED SUPPORT STRATEGIES TO IMPROVE PROGRESS

Strategy	Cost	Strength of evidence	Impact (months)
Feedback	£	✓✓✓	+8
Metacognition and self-regulation	£	✓✓✓✓	+7
Reading comprehension strategies	£	✓✓✓✓	+6
Collaborative learning	£	✓✓✓✓	+5
Oral language interventions	£	✓✓✓✓	+5
Peer tutoring	£	✓✓✓✓	+5
Mastery learning	£	✓✓✓	+5
Homework (secondary)	£	✓✓	+5
One to one tuition	££££	✓✓✓✓	+5
Phonics	£	✓✓✓✓✓	+4

When you have identified any strategies that are likely to improve school-wide practice, the next step is to look at the data for inconsistent results, or consistently poor results between pupils and any more specific patterns across the department/school.

> **Are there patterns in a particular group of pupils not achieving to the expected level?**
>
> **Meet with colleagues to discuss and agree sharing best practice through CPD and pupil intervention.**

> **Staff** In-Service Education and Training **(INSET)** **(e.g. guidance provided at staff meeting/activities during INSET) needs to be put in place to help the team raise the quality or implement a more effective pace to teaching and learning.**

If the issue is pupil related, consider the following:

ISSUE	SOLUTION	METHOD
Absence from lessons	Complete the missed work after school	Online work/Catch up programme
Inability to answer questions	Revision/exam practice/targeted intervention	Revision groups/practice tests/study-buddy
Insufficient work completed	Opportunities to catch up	Catch up programme/One-to-one support/small group work

Having a strong programme of general support available to them ensures that pupils do not slip too far behind and continue to make sufficient progress.

Last but not least, when you have identified any strategies that are likely to improve progress for key groups of pupils, the next step is to look at the inconsistent results of an individual teacher.

> **For each individual teacher, are there patterns in a particular group of pupils not achieving to the expected level?**
>
> **Meet with colleagues to discuss and agree any necessary staff training and pupil intervention.**
>
> **Focused CPD (e.g. peer observation, team teaching, or specific training) needs to be put in place to help the team raise the quality or implement a more effective pace to teaching and learning.**

For those pupils and staff underachieving for the first time, implement the actions as suggested in October. For those pupils and staff who are continuing to underachieve, implement an individual support plan as suggested in September.

> **(Senior leaders)   Update all plans and CPD**
>
> *Securing progress by checking we are achieving our targets and implementing improvements*

Updating the FIP, SIP, and SEF is the next formal evaluation of the year and will be the foundation for your report to the Senior Leadership Team (SLT) or Governors. Swift action to redress any issues is essential. Before completing the plans and forms, consider the following:

- Have you clearly articulated what you and others need to do, and when and where regarding updating the FIP/SIP/SEF?

- Have you given people involved in the process an opportunity to feedback and give their views as to what they think is going well and what could be improved?

- What is the deadline for the work to be completed?

- What clear milestones are to be reached along the way and are they being met?

- If the milestones are not being met, what action is being taken to redress this?

- Have you included updating the statutory areas of Behaviour/Attendance/ SEN (including the Education and Health Care Plans – EHCPs)/LAC (Looked After Children)/Behaviour/Attendance/Safeguarding/Careers?

- Have you cross-checked your actions against the latest inspection criteria and that you are Ofsted ready?

- What should people do if there is a problem?

- How and when are you going to follow up with the information that is recorded?

- What leadership and teaching CPD implications arise from this update?

 (Senior leaders) **Send off Capital bids**

Securing progress through improving the learning environment

It is now time to send off your bid for significant amounts of funding. Before pressing "send", consider the following:

- Have you clearly linked your strategic three-to-five-year plan to the work being bid for?

- Have you incorporated all the necessary consultations?

- Is the proposal as professional as it could be?

- How is what is being proposed the best for the pupils?

- Is what is being proposed workable?

- Have you piloted your proposal with a few trusted colleagues and received feedback?

- Have you gone through it yourself and checked everything against the success criteria?

> **(All leaders) Celebrate a term (well) done**
>
> *Securing progress through recognising and celebrating the progress made over the autumn term*

Just before you crack open a bottle of something to celebrate the end of this longest term, there is one final job that needs to be done: Sign off the progress of the trainee and new teachers on their support programme for the autumn term. Key questions that will help evaluate this include the following:

Attendance and punctuality: Has their attendance/punctuality rate been high or dropped below expectation?

Professionalism: Have they behaved in line with the school's Code of Conduct, or have there been issues?

Teachers' Standards: Is there sufficient evidence to say they are on track to successfully meet the standards?

Evidence: Has someone checked that all the evidence that should be in place is in place?

Concerns: Are there any concerns that need addressing in the spring term?

Once all is in order, these need to be signed off and sent to the local authority/ relevant training body and a celebration of the progress the trainee/new teachers have made this term should be had.

Celebrate

Arrange a method of celebrating success: Whether this is through presentations or competitions, giving out prizes in assembly or at a staff meeting, publishing social media posts, or a press release or article for the school's newsletter/website, create an opportunity to celebrate your school's success over the autumn term and make explicit the progress you are making as a school.

Moments that count in December:Teamwork

When leadership is good, it is based more than anything else in the trust, mutual respect, and esprit du corps shared by the members of the team. This is seldom seen more than at the end of term, when there are many more events than usual, when other staff members, not to mention the pupils, can get tetchy to say the least, and it can often turn into silly season.

The last two weeks of a busy autumn term featured two Parents' Consultation Evenings, a concert, staff pantomime, an *evening Nine lessons and Carols and 2 in-school carol services.* The leadership team could feel rightly pleased with themselves as all had turned up to every event (it was the way with that team, despite not having to be at evening events, we preferred to turn out on mass and support each other). The end of term assembly was over, prizes awarded, songs sung, and all had gone off remarkably well. The team stood in the hall in a self-congratulatory manner – only an hour to go! We retired to the Head's study to share a mince pie or two before bidding goodbye to the pupils.

Then the fire alarm sounded – just what you need with the end of term.

According to the Head, the fate that awaited the perpetrator was exceptionally unpleasant. As we rushed out, we could smell smoke, the pupils dashed past, and two of us went to investigate. To our dismay the grand piano in the hall was on fire; who on Earth had let that happen? And then it dawned on us, that the last people in the hall were the entire leadership team, none of whom had thought to blow out the candles on the advent wreath. We took collective blame, privately and behind closed doors saw the funny side, and never breathed a word to anyone else.

December offers us all an opportunity, a moment that counts, to thank, recognise, and appreciate the contribution and commitment of the staff, pupils, parents, and the local community in supporting each other in our work and the pupils on their educational journey.

(Understandably) Anon.

Summary and checklist for December

LEADER ACTION	FOCUS	SENIOR LEADERS	MIDDLE LEADERS
Analyse and applaud	Results from end of term tests and reports written and recorded		
	Surveys/questionnaires for parents/staff and pupils		▓
Arrange	Arrange scheme of work (SOW) for Spring 1	▓	
Action	Begin work on Integrated Framework		▓
	Update Coursework, Catch Up, and Revision programmes		
	Update SEF/SIP/FIP, and CPD in light of data		
	Send off Capital bids		
	Celebrate a term (well) done		

Spring term: Nurturing growth

DOI: 10.4324/9781003129691-6

SPRING TERM SUMMARY				
KEY				
🕓 **Action that prepares future work**	⋙ **Action that supports current work**		👍 **Action that analyses, evaluates, and celebrates previous work**	
Statutory activity (higher priority)		**Non-statutory activity (lower priority)**		
A–Z of key school activities	**January**	**February**	**March**	**April**
Admissions			👍	
Capital bids			👍	
Census		⋙		
Coursework, Catch Up, and Revision programmes	⋙	⋙	⋙	⋙
End/start of term	👍		🕓 ⋙	👍
Exams and careers	⋙			🕓
Improvement Plans		⋙		⋙
Leavers	🕓			
Monitoring and tracking	⋙			⋙
Options	⋙		👍	
Parents' Evenings	⋙			
Performance appraisal and pay			⋙	
Pupil recruitment/destinations			👍	
Quality assurance		⋙		
Schemes of Work/Curriculum Maps		⋙	⋙	
Staff Handbook/Prospectus etc.				👍
Staff recruitment	⋙			
Tests		🕓	⋙	👍 🕓
Timetable			🕓	
Website and displays	⋙			⋙

January

January sees the psychological shift that sees the end of the academic year come into view and next year's intentions turn into this year's imperatives.

January should be experienced with focus and resolve.

DOI: 10.4324/9781003129691-7

Introduction: January

January provides the start to a new year and the psychological stimulus to work with refreshed vigour and renewed focus as the end of the academic year comes into direct view. Short-term actions are approached with renewed vigour and long-term plans are begun in earnest. Here is what lies ahead for the month of January.

JANUARY SUMMARY		
KEY		
(icon) **Action that prepares future work**	(icon) **Action that supports current work**	(icon) **Action that analyses, evaluates, and celebrates previous work**
Statutory activity (higher priority)		**Non-statutory activity (lower priority)**
Action	*Leaders*	*School focus for January*
(thumbs up icon)	All leaders	Evaluate end of term and start of term arrangements
(arrows icon)	Senior leaders	Begin staffing for the next academic year
(arrows icon)	All leaders	Finalise exam entries and start Options process (KS4 and 5)
(arrows icon)	All leaders	Implement spring monitoring and tracking
(arrows icon)	All leaders	Update Coursework, Catch Up, and Revision programmes
(arrows icon)	All leaders	Update website and displays
(arrows icon)	All leaders	Begin Parents' Evenings
(clock icon)	All leaders	Finalise exam entries and leavers plans

As the new year and the new term starts, create an opportunity at your next leadership team/department meeting to discuss the following standing agenda items:

- **Staffing and safeguarding**: Are there any staffing and/or safeguarding concerns to be urgently addressed this month?

- **Calendar**: Are there any pinch points this month which need to be carefully managed beforehand?

- **Trips and school activities**: Are there any trips or large group activities this month, or during the February half term, which need to be carefully managed?

- **Website and communications**: Is the website up to date and are parents/pupils/staff clear about what is happening this month? Is there robust, challenging, and engaging online work available for pupils to complete if needed?

- **Inspection ready**: Which areas need addressing this month to ensure we are on track with our work?

The rationale for the other actions taking place this month, and in this order, include that an action is *more important* or needs doing *more urgently*, has a higher priority and therefore comes earlier in the month and vice versa. An action may be *part of a process* and so must happen before one action, but after another. Also, certain actions are *fixed* to events outside of the school's control and so these actions are tied to a particular date in the calendar (for example, external exams) or are actions *related to a fixed* event. Thus, an evaluation and celebration of the end of term/start of term arrangements must take place in early January.

The new year sees the work of the school getting straight back into action with the recruitment of new staff for the next academic year, the signing off of exam entries, the start of the options process, and the checking on the progress of pupil work, especially coursework and any support/intervention programmes. As we are a third of the way through the year, this is a good opportunity to ensure the website is fully up to date and to spruce up tired-looking displays ahead of the annual round of parents' evenings.

Looking ahead, it is time to also ensure that the road ahead, for those to be leaving the school this year, is as well-structured and supportive as possible, and so dusting down those school leavers plans is the last on the list for January.

 (All leaders)   **Evaluate the end and start of terms**

Securing progress through a continued, consistent focus on teaching and learning

A new year, a new term, and a fresh start. Here is an opportunity to reinforce key messages and routines. Before diving into the new term, take a moment to reflect on and confirm how well things were drawn to a close last term, and how well things have settled into place this term. This is also the month when applications for Reception places closes, so for primary schools, ensure any last-minute questions are fully answered.

Analyse

■ Report on attendance data – any issues to address/follow up?

■ How does this data compare to previous years, and the latest local and national benchmarks?

■ How effectively delivered and successful was the new staff/pupil induction?

■ What positive messages about learning, teaching, and leadership come out of the end of term/start of term?

■ What learning for pupils, teachers, and leaders come out of the end of term/start of term?

Evaluate

■ What do you understand to be the reasons behind any successes? Can these be developed?

■ What do you understand to be the reasons behind any areas that were less successful? How are these going to be addressed and resolved?

Action

■ What follow-up actions need to be made/key messages need to be communicated as a result of your analysis/evaluation?

■ Primaries: What last-minute arrangements need to be made to follow up with prospective Reception parents?

Celebrate

■ Before moving on, spend a moment recognising and reinforcing the progress being demonstrated across the department/school in relation to effective routines, sending out key messages through tutor time, staff briefing, or an article for the school's newsletter/website.

■ Write letters of appreciation to key teachers and leaders for their notable positive contribution.

 (Senior leaders) **Begin staff recruitment**

Securing the best teachers to elicit the best learning and progress from pupils

Ensuring the pupils are being taught, led, and supported by the best staff is critical to the pupils' progress and success. This can be a very time-consuming activity.

Having all the documentation and resources needed, right from the start, will ensure no false starts and everyone can get on with the job of delivering a high-quality education from the first. Before you get going with recruiting staff, use the following to help check that you have covered all the actions that are needed for staff recruitment to be a success. An electronic copy of this recruitment checklist can be found and downloaded from the School Leader's Resources page at: www.schoolleaderdevelopment.com.

INTERVIEW PROCESS INCLUDING SAFEGUARDING PROCEDURES

1	Reply to any resignations and if necessary, arrange exit interviews	Start
2	Agree selection criteria	Three weeks before
3	Design Job Description/Person Specification	Three weeks before
4	Advertise post, including information on safeguarding	Three weeks before
5	Choose method of selection/assessment	Two weeks before
6	Design interview questions	Two weeks before
7	Put together interview pack	Two weeks before
8	Send out interview pack	Two weeks before
9	Organise interview and agree selection criteria	Two weeks before
10	Brief staff; arrange and brief pupil panel(s)/school council	Two weeks before
11	Read applications and shortlist	Week before
12	Request references and ask for criminal records/self-disclosure	Week before
13	Organise refreshments/interview room etc.	Week before
14	Ask about any gaps in application and any disclosures	At the interview
15	Make decision – make conditional offer	After the interview
16	Check references, qualifications, and documents	Day after
17	Request Disclosure and Barring Service (DBS) and prohibition order check	Day after
18	Update Single Central Register	Day after

 (All leaders) Confirm exam entries / start Options
Securing progress through ensuring that the best curriculum choices are made by the pupils

For secondary schools, with both Sixth Form applications for universities and the deadline to confirm exam entries ahead of the examinations in the summer due out this month, January is an important month. Liaise with your team and the exams officer early, so that any sensitive conversations needing to be had with staff, pupils, or parents can be had, with agreements being reached sooner rather than later.

Following discussions from the integrated framework last term, the curriculum proposals available to put to pupils should be clearer. For help in organising an Options Evening, see the Open Evening checklist in September or the Parents' Evening checklist in October. Ahead of that process beginning, use the following to help ensure that the process is as effective as possible.

- Have you clearly articulated what you and others need to do, and when and where regarding options?

- What are the key deadlines for the work to be completed?

- If there are additional things for people to do, what should they do about covering their other work that is being missed?

- What should people do if there is a problem?

Here is a list of key information that needs to be in place from the start of the options process. A member of the Senior Leadership Team (SLT) should ensure that all of this information is ready, available, and accessible before the project goes live. An electronic copy of this options checklist can be found and downloaded from the School Leader's Resources page at: www.schoolleaderdevelopment.com.

TASKS	JANUARY	FEBRUARY	MARCH
Review labour market information (LMI) to inform options			
Carry out options survey/curriculum audit to scope courses			
Review and agree the curriculum offer			
Outline curriculum and options process to stakeholders			
Carry out consultation of curriculum offer			
Consult pupil groups in registration			
Confirm options offer with leadership team			
Confirm options offer with Governors			
Update website with subject information			
Clarify options process at staff In-Service Education and Training (INSET)			
Arrange Heads of Faculty to present subjects			
Distribute Options Booklet for review and amending			
Distribute final Options Booklet and guidance			
Arrange taster sessions/presentations			
Options Booklet return deadline			
Communicate Options guidance at Parents' Evening			
Arrange Options Evening and distribute options forms			
Arrange and communicate Options surgeries			
Option forms returned from …			
Option forms returned – final deadline …			
Collate the list in Excel			
See pupils needing changes			
Communicate final options list			

(All leaders)   Spring monitoring and tracking in place

Securing progress by routinely checking that everyone is making expected progress

The need to observe the areas over which we lead and report on progress continues. Here are some questions to help ensure your monitoring tracking is as rigorous as it needs to be in January:

- Have you clearly articulated what you and others need to do, and when and where regarding monitoring and tracking teaching and learning?

- Have you clearly articulated how staff/pupils' work will benefit as a result of what you are asking people to do?

- What are the key deadlines for the work to be completed?

- If there are additional things for people to do, what should they do about covering their other work that is being missed?

- What should people do if there is a problem?

This is also a good time following the end of term tests and mock exams to check more specifically how effective the school's assessment for learning techniques are being used in class (Gershon 2009). When quality assuring the work of teachers in lessons, look specifically at how effectively the following are being used to aid and support progress in lessons. An electronic copy of this table with these and over 50 Assessment for Learning techniques can be found and downloaded from the School Leader's Resources page at: www.schoolleaderdevelopment.com.

ASSESSMENT FOR LEARNING STRATEGIES AND TECHNIQUES

Progress Focus	Assessment for Learning (AfL) techniques to observe
Aims and targets	Learning aims are clear in lessons, on lesson plans/Schemes of Work
	Learning targets are clear in lessons, plans, books, trackers, and teacher planners
Learning	Progress in learning is evident through, for example, an up-to-date learning journal, or longer, more accurate pieces of work in books
Knowledge and skills	Online interviews and presentations help demonstrate skills/knowledge
	Skills are more evident through "Practice and Demonstrate" activities
Questioning and answering	Questioning increasingly moves from teachers asking questions to pupils
	Questioning increasingly moves from closed to open questions
	Use of plenaries at end or mini plenaries during lessons
	More effective use of questioning by teacher, e.g. "pose, pause, pounce, bounce"

ASSESSMENT FOR LEARNING STRATEGIES AND TECHNIQUES

Progress Focus	Assessment for Learning (AfL) techniques to observe
Marking and feedback	Marking and feedback on work increasingly move from teacher to pupils
	Online polls – programmes such as Mentimeter aid learning and discussion
	Feedback – regular use of "2 stars and a wish"/"What went well (WWW)/Even Better If (EBI)" by teachers, groups, peers, and individual pupils
Assessments	Use of informal assessment, e.g. drag, and drop activities
	Use of quizzes, tests, and formal tests to check progress in learning
	Level/grade scores are evident in lessons, books, and lesson plans

Once you have gathered your data, use the following to help produce a robust and rigorous analysis of your findings:

■ **Target**: To what extent does current progress match the target you are aiming to achieve?

■ **Local/National benchmarks**: To what extent does current progress match the target achieved locally/nationally?

■ **Time frame**: To what extent are you on track?

■ **Milestones**: To what extent have you reached those milestones you wanted to reach?

■ **RAG rating**: Where in the data are things going better than expected (colour coded green), as expected (colour coded amber), and worse than expected (colour coded red) at this point in the year?

■ What **follow up actions** are needed as a result?

Update your spreadsheet and file of evidence.

Distribute examples of excellent work.

Arrange for updated communication to be sent/training put in place for issues that need addressing.

 (All leaders)   Review support in light of latest data

Securing progress by not letting anyone achieve anything less than their best

With the next round of whole school or department data coming through from the marks from the end of term tests comes an opportunity to celebrate and an opportunity to learn. For further guidance on data analysis, see September's

"Annual Exam Results". Results that are at, above, and beyond what you are expecting means the learning process, outlined below, is working very well and present a moment to celebrate and evaluate why that is – what great leadership, teaching, and learning are going on that can be shared?

---

10 strategies to build resilience in exams and tests

Following mock exams and tests, this is the perfect time to introduce exam preparation. Here are some strategies to support pupil performance in exams. Facilitate the pupils to:

Practice answering **all the questions set**.

Practice answering increasing numbers of questions **under timed conditions**.

Practice answering increasing numbers of questions **with word limits**.

Practice **using/reinforce key exam terminology** from a literacy mat/set of flash cards.

Have **annotated displays** to make expectations and standards explicit.

Use the **modelling rule of 3**: Teacher models the answer – whole class answers – individuals answer.

Use the **crib sheet rule of 3**: Answer question – with crib sheet – after reading crib sheet – without crib sheet.

Prepare for exams in **15-minute short bursts**, not hour-long stretches of time.

Use spacing; Revise the same information three or four times with a week's gap between each time.

Use interleaving: Revise a little of different topics to keep previously learnt work fresh.

Having a strong programme of general support available to them ensures that pupils do not slip too far behind and continue to make sufficient progress. Use the following checklist to check that you are supporting all pupils to achieve their potential:

- This month, have you checked that pupils with more than two days absence have completed all missed work?

- In your schemes of work, have you built in time to revise and test current and previously learnt work?

- For pupils who need additional support to catch up with their classwork or coursework, have you put a schedule of support in place and communicated this to staff, pupils, and parents?

However, results that are not what you are expecting means the learning process is not working as well as it could be and is an opportunity to carry out a gap analysis and urgently correct the trajectory of progress. The issue may be related to the leadership, the teaching, or the learning within the learning process. The table below illustrates some examples of this.

ISSUE	CHECK			
Inconsistent results between classes	Scheme of work	Programme of study	Assessment process	Quality of teaching
Inconsistent results for a pupil group	Prior attainment (High/Middle/Low)	Target grades (High/Middle/Low)	Groups (special educational needs – SEN/pupil premium – PP/ English as an Additional Language – EAL)	Gender (boys/girls)
Inconsistent results for a teacher	Pitch (Difficulty)	Pace (Adaptability)	Differentiation (Accessibility)	Engagement (Style)

If from the data there are inconsistent results between teachers, you must look at your own leadership practice first.

> How fit for purpose, clear, comprehensive, and coherent are your schemes of work and programmes of study (the what are we teaching and the when are we teaching it)?
>
> How often are you checking the quality of teaching and learning going on in your department's lessons, through, for example, learning walks and book scrutiny, and how often is that learning being effectively assessed (the how effective is the teaching)?

When you have identified any strategies that are likely to improve school-wide practice, the next step is to look at the data for inconsistent results, or consistently poor results between pupils and any more specific patterns across the department/school.

> **Are there patterns in a particular group of pupils not achieving to the expected level?**
> **Meet with colleagues to discuss and agree sharing best practice through continuing professional development (CPD) and pupil intervention.**
> **Staff INSET (e.g. guidance provided at staff meeting/activities during INSET) needs to be put in place to help the team raise the quality or implement a more effective pace to teaching and learning.**

If the issue is pupil related, consider the following:

ISSUE	SOLUTION	METHOD
Absence from lessons	Complete the missed work after school	Online work/Catch up programme
Inability to answer questions	Revision/exam practice/ targeted intervention	Revision groups/practice tests/ study-buddy
Insufficient work completed	Opportunities to catch up	Catch up programme/one-to-one support/small group work

Having a strong programme of general support available to them ensures that pupils do not slip too far behind and continue to make sufficient progress. Use the following checklist to check that you are supporting all pupils to achieve their potential:

Last but not least, when you have identified any strategies that are likely to improve progress for key groups of pupils, the next step is to look at the inconsistent results of an individual teacher.

> **For each individual teacher, are there patterns in a particular group of pupils not achieving to the expected level?**
> **Meet with colleagues to discuss and agree any necessary staff training and pupil intervention.**
> **Focused CPD (e.g. peer observation, team teaching, or specific training) needs to be put in place to help the team raise the quality or implement a more effective pace to teaching and learning.**

For those pupils and staff underachieving for the first time, implement the actions as suggested in October. For those pupils and staff who are continuing to underachieve, implement an individual support plan as suggested in September.

> ⟫⟫⟫ **(All leaders)**   **Update displays and website**
>
> *Securing progress by displaying work that celebrates and makes explicit high-quality learning*

This may seem like an additional job that is unnecessary, but to keep the working atmosphere fresh, any displays or website content that is out of date need to be removed and more up-to-date work displayed/posted. Consider the following to ensure your website/school walls continue to be interesting and stimulating:

- **Word walls** – displaying key words for pupils to incorporate into their work and conversations.
- **Annotated work** – displaying exemplar work that is annotated so pupils are clear what to do to achieve a particular grade.
- **Success criteria** – Key skills are displayed with descriptors as to what needs to be accomplished to achieve successively higher grades.
- **Subject Stars** – displaying photographs of pupils and their latest grades/ scores helps promote a sense of success/improvement.

Note: Make sure any displayed work is labelled with the creator's name and tutor or year group to help promote the sense of success and achievement.

Moments that count in January: Snow – putting the pupils first

When I was a deputy headteacher, the forecast that particular week in January was for snow.

The rest of the SLT were as excited as I was at the prospect of snow, manning the phones, moving into a state of emergency, and possibly, just maybe, having to go home due to snow. Thursday evening and the anticipated snow came, thick heaps of it. The leadership team were called to have a tour of the school and agree a plan of action. Against all our calls of Health and Safety (unsafe paths, what if the boiler broke down, etc.), the Headteacher always had an answer – we stay open as much as we can – the pupils' education must come first.

Fast forward a few years and my own headship and a similar scenario; touring the school with the leadership team ahead of a decision to close the school because of snow. I must admit to a small voice agreeing to the team's calls of Health and Safety (unsafe paths, what if the boiler broke down, etc.), but a stronger voice was heard by this headteacher, that had a recognisable answer – we stay open as much as we can – the pupils' education must come first.

Sometimes it is easy and sometimes it is hard as a leader to do what is right. This phrase sums up beautifully the touchstone for school leaders that can help us with those sometimes-difficult decisions:

I value you, and I will trust, empower, support, and challenge you. However, never ask me to put you before our children and their learning.

 (All leaders)   Start Parents' Evenings

Securing progress by getting everyone into good working/learning habits right from the start

Parents form the third side of the triangle between the school, pupils, and home. Having the parents on board is a significant advantage when working with the young people in our care. Parents' evenings are the time in the year when that relationship can be significantly developed. This is also another good time to send out the parent questionnaires that have just been created. See October for the Parents' Evening checklist to ensure you cover everything. Also use the following questions to help check that you have covered all the actions that are needed for parents' evenings to be a success:

▧ Have you clearly articulated what you and others need to do, and when and where regarding parents' evenings?

▧ What are the deadlines for the work to be completed?

▧ If this is additional to people's work (e.g. part-time staff who aren't usually in school on those days), what should they do about covering their other work that is being missed, compensating them for additional work?

▧ What should people do if there is a problem?

▧ Ensure you distribute and collect in the evaluation forms.

▧ Follow up with any parents that were not able to attend.

 (All leaders)   Finalise exam entries and leavers plans

Securing progress by having clear, ambitious goals for our pupils

With Year 6, Year 11, and Year 13 being the most important year groups to the school and as their results reflect on the quality of education they receive at the

school, attention must be turned to ensuring the school finalises the best exam/
test entry level for the pupils and effectively supports them in their transition to
the next stage of their education, employment, or training.

To help prepare the best leavers events, explore what others have written or
are doing. The Department for Education (DfE) and companies such as Teachwire
and Twinkl offer some useful insights and on their websites give some useful
guidance. More information on these can be found in Chapter 15 at the end of
this book. Also, use online tools such as Google Docs or Google Sheets to work
on key documents or data concurrently with your team and ensure you work as
effectively as possible. Here are some points to help ensure the pupils go on to the
best and most appropriate destination of choice:

- Have you discussed and agreed the final exam entries with pupils, staff, and
  parents?

- Have these been communicated to the exam boards by the set deadline?

- Have you clearly articulated what you and others need to do, and when and
  where regarding exams and careers with Year 6, Year 11, or Year 13?

- What clear milestones are to be reached along the way?

- If this is additional to people's work, what should they do about covering their
  other work that is being missed?

- What should people do if there is a problem?

Summary and checklist for January

LEADER ACTION	FOCUS	SENIOR LEADERS	MIDDLE LEADERS
Analyse and applaud	End of term and start of term arrangements		
Action	Begin staff recruitment for the next academic year		
	Confirmed exam entries and started the Options process		
	Implement Spring monitoring and tracking		
	Update Coursework, Catch Up, and Revision programmes		
	Update website and displays		
	Begin Parents' Evenings		
Prepare	Finalise exam entries and leavers plans		

February

February, the mid-point of the academic year, is the metaphorical turning of the tides as teaching continues to move forwards at pace and at the same time, previous learning needs to be revised or caught up.

It is where meaningful accountability can be applied to leaders, teachers, and pupils to create a stronger sense of urgency to the work at hand.

February should be experienced with calm realism.

DOI: 10.4324/9781003129691-8

Introduction: February

To some extent, February can feel like a re-run of previous months; more curriculum coverage with catching up and admin tasks to be completed. Where February differs is in the volume of learning now to be carried and the proximity of that weight to the exam season. This creates more of a sense of urgency than panic, as there is time (just) still ahead.

FEBRUARY SUMMARY					
KEY					
👍	Action that analyses, evaluates, and celebrates previous work	⟫⟫	Action that supports current work	🕐	Action that prepares future work
Statutory activity (higher priority)			**Non-statutory activity (lower priority)**		
Action	*Leaders*	*School Focus for February*			
⟫⟫	All leaders	Complete and return the spring term census			
⟫⟫	All leaders	Quality assurance – spring programme starts			
⟫⟫	All leaders	Update Coursework, Catch Up, and Revision programmes			
⟫⟫	All leaders	Update School Evaluation Form (SEF)/School Improvement Plan (SIP)/Faculty Improvement Plan (FIP), and continuing professional development (CPD) in light of mid-year data			
🕐	Middle leaders	Update the schemes of work for Spring 2/curriculum maps			
🕐	All leaders	Arrange mid-year/end of term assessments			

As February starts, create an opportunity at your next leadership team/department meeting to discuss the following standing agenda items:

- **Staffing and safeguarding**: Are there any staffing and/or safeguarding concerns to be urgently addressed this month? How are options choices progressing? What early implications are there for next year?

- **Calendar**: Are there any pinch points this month which need to be carefully managed beforehand?

- **Trips and school activities**: Are there any trips or large group activities this month which need to be carefully managed, especially at half term?

- **Website and communications**: Is the website up to date and are parents/pupils/staff clear about what is happening this month? Is there robust, challenging, and engaging online work available for pupils to complete if needed?

- **Inspection ready**: Which areas need addressing this month to ensure we are on track with our work?

The rationale for the other actions taking place this month, and in this order, include that an action is *more important* or needs doing *more urgently*, has a higher priority and therefore comes earlier in the month and vice versa. An action may be *part of a process* and so must happen before one action, but after another. Also, certain actions are *fixed* to events outside of the school's control and so these actions are tied to a particular date in the calendar (for example, external exams) or are actions *related to a fixed* event.

With February comes the spring term census and the second round of quality assurance, ideally, bringing both internal and external expertise to check that the quality of the work in the school is as good as it should be. The monthly check on coursework, revision, and those who are not achieving as well as they could be continues apace and enables all leaders to update their plans and CPD programmes.

This mid-year checking also enables middle leaders to accurately prepare and update their Schemes of Work for the second half of the spring term, as everything should be reading "Full Steam Ahead!" in preparation for the second round of end of term tests.

 (All leaders)   Complete the spring term census

Securing progress by ensuring everyone has the most up-to-date information on pupils.

Having (successfully!) run this process in October, everything should be in place for a smoother, more efficient data gathering process this month. As this census is the data used to allocate funding, it is essential it is as accurate as possible. Ahead of actioning work on the census, spend a short time preparing the groundwork:

- Consult the latest guidance on the census for any updates/changes (see Chapter 15 for useful websites).

- Is everyone involved at the various stages prepared and ready?

- Are you clear and have you communicated to relevant staff what needs to happen, as well as by when and by whom?

- What are the biggest challenges that lie ahead and how are those challenges going to be met?

- From the data, what are the key messages that need to be communicated to staff, leaders, and Governors?

- Keep it flexible: Once your proposal is live, welcome feedback on what is going well and how it could be improved further.

 (All leaders)   Quality assurance – Spring programme starts

Securing progress by others internally or externally checking that what we do is best practice

---

At this point in the year, the second round of quality assurance checks to see that what should be in place, is in place. Before taking action and quality assuring your department's or your school's work, consider the following points to help ensure that what you continue to do is fit for purpose and effective. Having a different pair of internal eyes where there are no concerns should be sufficient. However, where concerns have been growing, it is imperative that external quality assurance is used to check the quality of work taking place in the school and either way, answer the question, is what we say in our intention being implemented? Here are a number of methods by which we can quality assure the work of the department or the school.

- Monitoring – questionnaires, observations, book looks, displays

- Tracking – spreadsheets, data analysis, patterns

- Audits

- Feedback – individual or group interviews/evaluations with students, staff, or parents

- Monitoring and tracking schedules

- Learning walks

- Logs

- Minutes of meetings

- Observations and feedback

- Other quality assurance (internal) – other teachers, school leaders, and Governors

- Other quality assurance (external) – specialist leaders from the Master of Arts in Teaching (MAT), Local Education Authority (LEA), or local university/ training body

Use these to provide evidence that the methods by which leaders lead, teachers teach, and pupils learn are optimal. Where learning, teaching, and leadership is sub-optimal, this needs to be identified, reported with the sharing of best practice, e.g. in staff In-Service Education and Training (INSET)/CPD, and a plan of action. See September and October for more details.

Moments that count: School trips

Whilst at sixth form in the late nineties studying for my A-levels the history department organised a history trip to Berlin, not one of my friendship group was studying history and I was extremely nervous about going on a trip with a group of my classmates that I barely knew but I also really, really wanted to go as I loved the subject and had never been abroad anywhere before.

The trip was fantastic but the bit I remember the most was our trip to Sachsenhausen Memorial and Museum on the site of the former concentration camp. It was a sunny day and our teacher led us out to the roll call area and began to explain what would have taken place here every morning; as he talked the sun disappeared behind a cloud and the birds fell silent, we stood there, a group of 35 17–18 years olds in complete silence feeling, for perhaps the first time, the enormity of what had happened here and feeling an emotional connection with the events of the past.

This moment has never left me and in 2008 I ran my first overseas A-Level trip. There was no doubt in my mind where we would go. All the excited pupil-talk beforehand had been of who they would be sharing with, shopping and whether or not the teachers would allow them to have drink, just as it had been for me years before, and I began to worry that perhaps I had bitten off more than I could chew! But I had not needed to worry, they were a wonderful group of pupils and we had a great time.

Then came the day that we visited Sachsenhausen. This time I led them out to the roll call area and as we walked a hush began to descend over our group and I could see in their faces that they were feeling the same way that I had years before. We stopped and stood in silent reflection as it began to pour with rain. That is the moment that counted.

I have been on numerous educational visits and when done well the importance of these never fails to amaze me, whether the trip's purpose is for academic reasons, a team building day for the new Year 7's or a cultural experience in another country these are the moments that our pupils will cherish. The school year is busy and time is precious but it is important to invest in these kinds of experiences; the learning that takes place is difficult to replicate within the classroom – listen to your pupils, former pupils, your own children and even your friends when they talk about their school day, many of the stories they will tell will begin "Do you remember that trip when…"

Clare Smith, Assistant Headteacher

> **⟫⟫⟫** **(All leaders)** **Review support in light of latest data**
>
> *Securing progress by not letting anyone achieve anything less than their best*

The latest round of whole school or department data coming through from the latest assessments presents an opportunity to celebrate and an opportunity to learn. Results that are at, above, and beyond what you are expecting means the learning process, outlined below, is working very well and present a moment to celebrate and evaluate why that is – what great leadership, teaching, and learning is going on that can be shared?

However, results that are not what you are expecting means the learning process is not working as well as it could be and presents an opportunity to carry out a gap analysis and urgently correct the trajectory of progress. The issue may be related to the leadership, the teaching, or the learning within the learning process. The table below illustrates some examples of this.

ISSUE	CHECK			
Inconsistent results between classes	Scheme of work	Programme of study	Assessment process	Quality of teaching
Inconsistent results for a pupil group	Prior attainment (High/Middle/Low)	Target grades (High/Middle/Low)	Groups (special educational needs – SEN/pupil premium – PP/English as an Additional Language – EAL)	Gender (boys/girls)
Inconsistent results for a teacher	Pitch (Difficulty)	Pace (Adaptability)	Differentiation (Accessibility)	Engagement (Style)

If from the data there are inconsistent results between teachers, consider the Education Endowment Foundation (EEF)'s guidance (2018) to see if the school needs to make improvements to the teaching and learning experience.

EDUCATION ENDOWMENT FOUNDATION'S TOP 10 RECOMMENDED SUPPORT STRATEGIES TO IMPROVE PROGRESS

Strategy	Cost	Strength of evidence	Impact (months)
Feedback	£	✓✓✓	+8
Metacognition and self-regulation	£	✓✓✓✓	+7
Reading comprehension strategies	£	✓✓✓✓	+6
Collaborative learning	£	✓✓✓✓	+5
Oral language interventions	£	✓✓✓✓	+5
Peer tutoring	£	✓✓✓✓	+5
Mastery learning	£	✓✓✓	+5
Homework (secondary)	£	✓✓	+5
One to one tuition	££££	✓✓✓✓	+5
Phonics	£	✓✓✓✓✓	+4

When you have identified any strategies that are likely to improve school-wide practice, the next step is to look at the data for inconsistent results, or consistently poor results between pupils and any more specific patterns across the department/school.

> **Are there patterns in a particular group of pupils not achieving to the expected level?**
>
> **Meet with colleagues to discuss and agree sharing best practice through CPD and pupil intervention.**
>
> **Staff INSET (e.g. guidance provided at staff meeting/activities during INSET) needs to be put in place to help the team raise the quality or implement a more effective pace to teaching and learning.**

If the issue is pupil related, consider the following:

ISSUE	SOLUTION	METHOD
Absence from lessons	Complete the missed work after school	Online work/Catch up programme
Inability to answer questions	Revision/exam practice/ targeted intervention	Revision groups/practice tests/ study-buddy
Insufficient work completed	Opportunities to catch up	Catch up programme/1-to-1 support/small group work

Having a strong programme of general support available to them ensures that pupils do not slip too far behind and continue to make sufficient progress.

Last but not least, when you have identified any strategies that are likely to improve progress for key groups of pupils, the next step is to look at the inconsistent results of an individual teacher.

> For each individual teacher, are there patterns in a particular group of pupils not achieving to the expected level?
>
> Meet with colleagues to discuss and agree any necessary staff training and pupil intervention.
>
> Focused CPD (e.g. peer observation, team teaching, or specific training) needs to be put in place to help the team raise the quality or implement a more effective pace to teaching and learning.

For those pupils and staff underachieving for the first time, implement the actions as suggested in October. For those pupils and staff who are continuing to underachieve, implement an individual support plan as suggested in September.

⟫ (All leaders) Update all plans and CPD

Securing progress by checking we are achieving our targets and implementing improvements.

As we are halfway through the year, updating the FIP, SIP and SEF is important as this will be the foundation for your next report to the Senior Leadership Team (SLT) or Governors and evidence you are Ofsted ready. Swift action to redress any issues is essential. Before completing the plans and forms, consider the following:

- Have you clearly articulated what you and others need to do, and when and where regarding updating your plan?
- Have you given people involved in the process an opportunity to feedback and give their views as to what they think is going well and what could be improved?
- What is the deadline for the work to be completed?
- What clear milestones are to be reached along the way and are they being met?
- If the milestones are not being met, what action is being taken to redress this?
- Have you included updating the statutory areas of Behaviour/Attendance/ SEN (including the Education and Health Care Plans – EHCPs)/LAC (Looked After Children)/Behaviour/Attendance/Safeguarding/Careers?
- Have you cross-checked your actions against the latest inspection criteria and that you are Ofsted ready?
- What should people do if there is a problem?
- How and when are you going to follow up with the information that is recorded?
- What leadership and teaching CPD implications arise from this update?

(Middle leaders)   Update Schemes of Work for Spring 2

Securing progress by designing a curriculum that is comprehensive, clear, and achievable

As you review/prepare your scheme of work for the end of the spring term, use the following to check it is as good as it can be:

- Are the **aims** of the scheme of work and each lesson **realistically high, clearly articulated**, and **ordered coherently** so progress over the scheme of work is **explicit**?

- Is the work to be completed **manageable, challenging**, and **consistently focused on pupil learning**?

- Is there explicit **progression in understanding** from description and facts to analysis and reasoning?

- Is there a clear **increase in the challenge/complexity of knowledge and skills** being learnt?

- Is the work expected to be completed **increasingly longer and harder**?

- Are activities progressing **from the class/group** to the **individual** over time and do they **include homework**?

- Is the **assessment for learning built into each lesson** and does it move **from informal to formal assessment?**

- What **provisions are in place** should anyone fall behind, or finish sooner than expected?

This is also the time of year to begin a full review of your curriculum maps. Below is a potted guide to help ensure your curriculum maps are as good as they can be.

A curriculum map is a thematic guide to the curriculum and what will be taught throughout the school. It will not tell you what will be taught lesson by lesson, nor what the learning aims and outcomes are. It is simply an overview as to what will be taught (Harpham 2020). With an increase in emphasis by school inspectors on the presence of a clear and coherent curriculum intent, it is essential that school leaders have curriculum maps and schemes of work consistently in place for all curriculum areas (Ofsted 2019b). Key points to bear in mind when constructing curriculum maps are given below.

Any curriculum map should be checked for being clear, comprehensive, and coherent.

Clear

- Begin with the end in mind: Is the outcome for each topic clear?
- Summarise key learning: Are the skills and knowledge being learnt in each topic clear?

Comprehensive

- Miss nothing: Does every subject teach everything that is required by law/the exam boards?

Coherent

- Build up skills and knowledge: Order topics to support subsequent topics for each subject.
- Connect skills and knowledge: Time topics to occur with similar topics at that time in other subjects.
- Can any topics be studied at another time of the year and be more effective (more coherent) as a result?

Further guidance can be found and downloaded from the School Leader's Resources page at: www.schoolleaderdevelopment.com or other useful websites, including The Key or the *Times Educational Supplement* (TES).

》》》 (All leaders) Arrange mid-year/end of term assessments

Securing progress through arranging an assessment of what has been learnt so far

In arranging the mid-year/ end of term assessments, it should be clear from the programme of study and scheme of work what learning needs to be assessed. Before you start the process of arranging the assessments, use the following to ensure the process is as effective as it can be.

Assessment preparation for teachers

In preparing pupils for their mid-year/end of term assessments, here are ten effective strategies that provide good value for money for teachers to ensure their pupils are assessment ready.

 Peer quizzes: Pupils quiz each other on what has been learnt so far and mark/ grade each other.

- Pupils revise and teacher tests previously learnt and current work, using online programmes such as Quizlet.

- Have pupils explain why an answer is right *and* why an answer is wrong.

- Use flash cards to focus pupils' minds on key terms and concepts, using online resources such as Kahoot.

- Develop exam stamina by training pupils to revise in short, intensive sessions and answer questions over longer periods of time.

- Use past papers to develop pupil exam vocabulary.

- Have pupils use Mind Maps to organise complex/detailed projects.

- Have pupils use Literacy Maps to encapsulate key terms and concepts.

- Use Spaced Retrieval in schemes of work to keep previously learnt work fresh in pupils' minds.

- Do not accept classwork or homework that is below expectation from pupils. Have them re-draft and re-submit.

Assessment preparation for leaders

In arranging the mid-year/end of term assessments, confirm the process of assessment with school leaders and the exams officer and publicise.

Use the following to help prepare your end of term assessments:

- Ensure all pupils have target grades given to them for each subject.

- Ensure all pupils and parents know those target grades.

- Ensure all books/files have a completed tracker sheet that records test results through the year.

- Consistently prepare staff and pupils for the tests, consulting and communicating agreed expectations.

- Present the process to the SLT and heads of department, so everyone is clear on the process and key deadlines.

- Discuss with the SLT/Governors as to how the process is to be quality assured and how to ensure that the information being presented is accurate and that staff are consistent in how the assessments are being carried out and data recorded.

- Set up a Question Analysis spreadsheet and discuss results at the next department meeting.

- Set up a whole school data analysis spreadsheet and discuss results at the next SLT meeting.

Moments that count throughout the year:
It is always all about the pupils

Each year the children at my school cannot wait for World Book Day. At the end of February, you begin to hear the excited chatter in the playground and the big question "Who are you going to come as?" echoes round the corridors. When the big day finally arrives a colourful cast of Harry and Hermiones, superheroes and Gangsta Grannies parade in all their finery around the playground.

This year that day culminated with a member of the Senior Leadership Team reading to one of the classes, "Good luck" the Year 3 class teacher called over her shoulder as she left the classroom and I pondered upon her choices of words, but not for long as thirty expectant faces looked up at me in excited anticipation. I took my seat at the front "Hello everyone my name is Mrs Smith and I have come today to read you a story". Immediately six hands shot up into the air and I had not even asked a question! I then foolishly answered one pupil's question and then found myself with a never-ending sea of hands and questions ranging from "How many pages are there in the book?" to "Do you like pink?".

After this question I set a new rule "no questions until the end but the whole class could only ask three questions". After this we were able to get on with the story and despite the fact that the children were inching closer and closer with each word to the point where one little lad was sitting on my feet we reached the end, the children had listened brilliantly and I was looking forward to hearing their views on the story. "You can now ask three questions" I said and immediately Rosie raised her hand, "Rosie is this a really good question?" I said, "Yes Miss" she replied earnestly, "Remember the whole class is only allowed to ask three questions so do you think the other children will think it is a really good question Rosie?", "Yes, yes" was her frantic reply, "Great ask me your question Rosie". ...

"Can I go to the toilet?" The other children fell about laughing and I knew there was no way back from this and joined in!

Taking a leadership role in a school will inevitably take you away from the classroom and the higher you go the more this will happen, and the longer you are there the more you will forget. It is essential that you reconnect with your pupils.

They are at the heart of everything that we do and in the demanding and time-consuming role as a school leader we can sometimes lose sight of why we do what we do. Challenge yourself to spend a whole day in the classroom; I guarantee it will not be one that you forget in a hurry!

Clare Smith, Assistant Headteacher

Summary and checklist for February

LEADER ACTION	FOCUS	SENIOR LEADERS	MIDDLE LEADERS
Action	Complete and return the spring term census		
	Quality assurance – spring programme starts		
	Update Coursework, Catch Up, and Revision programmes		
	Update SEF/SIP/FIP, and CPD in light of mid-year data		
Arrange	Update scheme of work (SOW) for Spring 2		
	Arrange end of term assessments		

March

Spring!

March is where life in school moves up a gear. Finances and options are confirmed; coursework completion and final exams come within touching distance.

March is a month to be experienced with super-organisation.

DOI: 10.4324/9781003129691-9

Introduction: March

March is not the end, it is not the beginning of the end, but it is the end of the beginning. March feels like the final rehearsals ahead of a performance. There is an intensity, a complexity, and an urgency in the air, unlike any other month so far, like February, but without the luxury of time. Here is what you have ahead of you in March.

MARCH SUMMARY		
KEY		
👍 Action that analyses, evaluates, and celebrates previous work	⏰ Action that supports current work	🕐 Action that prepares future work
Statutory activity (higher priority)		**Non-statutory activity (lower priority)**

Action	Leaders	School focus for March
🕐	Senior leaders	Begin timetable for next year
🕐	All leaders	Prepare end of term and start of term arrangements
⏰	All leaders	Implement mid-year Performance Appraisal Review
⏰	All leaders	Complete end of term assessments
⏰	All leaders	Update Coursework, Catch Up, and Revision programmes
⏰	Middle leaders	Update the Schemes of Work for Summer 1
👍	Senior leaders	Evaluate admission arrangements/pupil recruitment
👍	Senior leaders	Evaluate finances and Capital bids
👍	All leaders	Evaluate options process (KS4/5)
⏰	All leaders	Action end of term and start of term arrangements

As March starts, create an opportunity at your next leadership team/department meeting to discuss the following standing agenda items:

- **Staffing and safeguarding**: Are there any staffing and/or safeguarding concerns to be urgently addressed this month (see January for staff recruitment procedures)?

- **Calendar**: Are there any pinch points this month which need to be carefully managed beforehand, especially if Easter is particularly early? How is everyone feeling? Do any changes need to be made to help get everyone through?

- **Trips and school activities**: Are there any trips or large group activities this month, or during the Easter break, which need to be carefully managed?

- **Website and communications**: Is the website up to date and are parents/pupils/staff clear about what is happening this month? Is there robust, challenging, and engaging online work available for pupils to complete if needed?

- **Inspection ready**: Which areas need addressing this month to ensure we are on track with our work?

The rationale for the other actions taking place this month, and in this order, include that an action is *more important* or needs doing *more urgently,* has a higher priority and therefore comes earlier in the month and vice versa. An action may be *part of a process* and so must happen before one action, but after another. Also, certain actions are *fixed* to events outside of the school's control and so these actions are tied to a particular date in the calendar (for example, external exams) or are actions *related to a fixed* event.

With confirmation as to intake for September and data coming in as regards options, the work on the timetable for September can begin. Similarly, with the Easter holidays being a movable feast, it is prudent to consider the end of term and start of term arrangements sooner rather than later, as this can also include valuable support time in the Easter break.

Everyone moves up a gear in March as Performance Appraisals are reviewed, end of term tests are marked, and increasingly, for both primary and secondary schools, imminent coursework and any missed learning is caught up on. Middle leaders, ahead of the Easter break, ensure that the schemes of work for the summer term are also fit for purpose as a result.

March sees a number of circumstances coming to fruition which require analysis, evaluation, and celebration. These include, for secondary schools, admissions and pupil recruitment (for primary schools, this is next month) and results from capital bid submissions and the options process are returned.

All that is left to do is to celebrate another term done and manage the school through to a restful break.

(Senior leaders)   Initial timetable creation

Securing progress by knowing the school community works efficiently and effectively

The mechanism to determine who goes where and when and what they are going to do begins again!

A small piece of intellectual engineering seeks to be fit for purpose and provide a master plan of organisation and efficiency. To help prepare the best timetable, explore what others have written or are doing. Companies such as SIMS, MIST, and Timetabler offer some useful insights and on their websites give some useful guidance. More information on these can be found in Chapter 15 at the end of this book. Also, use online tools such as Google Docs or Google Sheets to work on key documents or data concurrently with your team and ensure you work as effectively as possible. Use the following questions to help you produce a strong, effective timetable:

- Are you clear and have communicated to relevant staff what needs to happen, and by when and by whom?

- What are the biggest challenges that lie ahead and how are those challenges going to be addressed?

- Save time: Get copies/model examples of what you want and amend it to what you need.

- Propose the best: Provide a proposal that incorporates research and shares best practice in what you do. Consider attending the latest training/continuing professional development (CPD) to ensure what you do is up to date.

- Keep it flexible: Once your proposal is live, welcome feedback on what is going well and how it could be improved further. Review and tweak accordingly.

 (All leaders)   Prepare the end and start of terms

Securing progress through a continued focus on teaching, learning, and making good progress

The end of the spring term is busy and with so much going on, the school can become disorganised and fractious and as a result, leadership needs to be highly responsive and super-organised for all eventualities. Use the following ahead of any communications to help inform the end of term/start of term arrangements to help keep the end and start of term focused and positive.

- Have "End of Term/Start of Term" as an agenda item and get as many views as is reasonable to ensure you get a strong understanding of what needs to be done to wrap up the term, specify any work to be done over the Easter break, and the start of the next term.

- Save time: Use last year's information/guidance that went out and amend it to what you need.

- Co-ordinate: Check what other schools are doing and if applicable, align your holidays with theirs.

- Propose the best: Provide a proposal that incorporates research and shares best practice in what you do.

- If needed, propose the most workable solution: Pilot your proposal with a few trusted colleagues to give you feedback on your proposal. This will ensure that your proposal is as successful as it can be.

- Keep it flexible: Once your proposal is live, welcome feedback on what is going well and how it could be improved further. Review and tweak accordingly. Put out the final version when ready.

 (All leaders)   Review all Performance Appraisals

Securing progress by holding all staff to account for their work

---

Having set objectives for the year ahead in October, March is a good point to pause and check to see how well progress is being made in achieving them. Here are a few suggestions to help:

- Have you clearly articulated what you and others need to do, and when and where regarding reviewing everyone's performance appraisal?

- Have you clearly articulated how staff/pupils' work will benefit as a result of what you are asking people to do?

- What is the deadline for the work to be completed?

- Monitoring – having an up-to-date tracking spreadsheet clearly identifying the staff, the paperwork they have received, and the deadline dates for the various stages of this process will help you keep track and in control of a very wide-ranging process.

    - All paperwork out (By early March)

    - All performance review meetings scheduled (first two weeks in March)

    - All completed and signed performance reviews returned (last two weeks in March)

    - A summary report for the Senior Leadership Team (SLT) and Governors drafted, including whole school CPD recommendations (first week in April)

All of this is time-consuming and therefore ensuring each step is rigorously followed up, ensures the sooner the completion of the next stage of the process.

 (All leaders)   Complete end of spring term assessments

Securing progress through recognising and reporting pupil progress in their assessments

To ensure every pupil is included and receives the results from their end of term assessments, use the following to check the process you have in place is robust and comprehensive.

- All pupils have received their latest grades.

- All parents have received an update and been given their child's latest grades.

- All books/files/tracker sheets and pupil records have been updated.

- A question analysis is underway by departments and put on the agenda for the next department meeting.

- Whole school data analysis is underway by SLT and put on the agenda for the next SLT meeting.

- SLT are following up to ensure all tests have been completed and all results have been recorded.

- SLT/Governors are quality assuring that the information being presented is accurate and that staff are consistent in how the assessments are being carried out and data recorded.

 (All leaders)   Review support in light of latest data

Securing progress by not letting anyone achieve anything less than their best

For primary schools and the SATs, and secondaries with GCSE and A-Levels imminent, with the latest round of whole school or department data coming through from the latest assessments and the Easter holidays comes an opportunity to celebrate and an opportunity to learn. Results that are at, above, and beyond what you are expecting means the learning process, outlined below, is working very well and is a moment to celebrate and evaluate why that is – what great leadership, teaching, and learning is going on that can be shared?

However, results that are not what you are expecting means the learning process is not working as well as it could be and is an opportunity to carry out a gap analysis and urgently correct the trajectory of progress. The issue may be related to the leadership, the teaching, or the learning within the learning process. The table below illustrates some examples of this.

ISSUE	CHECK			
Inconsistent results between classes	Scheme of work	Programme of study	Assessment process	Quality of teaching
Inconsistent results for a pupil group	Prior attainment (High/Middle/Low)	Target grades (High/Middle/Low)	Groups (special educational needs – SEN/pupil premium – PP/ English as an Additional Language – EAL)	Gender (boys / girls)
Inconsistent results for a teacher	Pitch (Difficulty)	Pace (Adaptability)	Differentiation (Accessibility)	Engagement (Style)

If from the data there are inconsistent results between teachers, consider the Education Endowment Foundation (EEF)'s guidance (2018) to see if the school needs to make improvements to the teaching and learning experience.

EDUCATION ENDOWMENT FOUNDATION'S TOP 10 RECOMMENDED SUPPORT STRATEGIES TO IMPROVE PROGRESS

Strategy	Cost	Strength of evidence	Impact (months)
Feedback	£	✓✓✓	+8
Metacognition and self-regulation	£	✓✓✓✓	+7
Reading comprehension strategies	£	✓✓✓✓	+6
Collaborative learning	£	✓✓✓✓	+5
Oral language interventions	£	✓✓✓✓	+5
Peer tutoring	£	✓✓✓✓	+5
Mastery learning	£	✓✓✓	+5
Homework (secondary)	£	✓✓	+5
One to one tuition	££££	✓✓✓✓	+5
Phonics	£	✓✓✓✓✓	+4

When you have identified any strategies that are likely to improve school-wide practice, the next step is to look at the data for inconsistent results, or consistently poor results between pupils and any more specific patterns across the department/school.

Are there patterns in a particular group of pupils not achieving to the expected level?

Meet with colleagues to discuss and agree sharing best practice through CPD and pupil intervention.

Staff In-Service Education and Training **(INSET) (e.g. guidance provided at staff meeting/activities during INSET) needs to be put in place to help the team raise the quality or implement a more effective pace to teaching and learning.**

If the issue is pupil related, consider the following:

ISSUE	SOLUTION	METHOD
Absence from lessons	Complete the missed work after school	Online work/Catch up programme
Inability to answer questions	Revision/exam practice/ targeted intervention	Revision groups/practice tests/ study-buddy
Insufficient work completed	Opportunities to catch up	Catch up programme/ one-to-one support/small group work

Having a strong programme of general support available to them ensures that pupils do not slip too far behind and continue to make sufficient progress. Use the upcoming Easter holidays to intensively implement these.

Last but not least, when you have identified any strategies that are likely to improve progress for key groups of pupils, the next step is to look at the inconsistent results of an individual teacher.

For each individual teacher, are there patterns in a particular group of pupils not achieving to the expected level?

Meet with colleagues to discuss and agree any necessary staff training and pupil intervention.

Focused CPD (e.g. peer observation, team teaching, or specific training) needs to be put in place to help the team raise the quality or implement a more effective pace to teaching and learning.

For those pupils and staff underachieving for the first time, implement the actions as suggested in October. For those pupils and staff who are continuing to underachieve, implement an individual support plan as suggested in September.

 (Middle leaders) **Update Schemes of Work for Summer 1**

Securing progress by providing a comprehensive, clear, and achievable curriculum

---

As you review/prepare your scheme of work for the summer term, use the following to check it is as good as it can be:

- Are the **aims** of the scheme of work and each lesson **realistically high, clearly articulated**, and **ordered coherently** so progress over the scheme of work is **explicit**?

- Is the work to be completed **manageable, challenging**, and **consistently focused on pupil learning**?

- Is there explicit **progression in understanding** from description and facts to analysis and reasoning?

- Is there a clear **increase in the challenge/complexity of knowledge and skills** being learnt?

- Is the work expected to be completed **increasingly longer and harder?**

- Are activities progressing **from the class/group** to the **individual** over time and do they **include homework**?

- Is **assessment for learning built into each lesson** and does it move **from informal to formal assessment**?

- What **provisions are in place** should anyone fall behind, or finish sooner than expected?

Moments that count in March: Teamwork and determination

When I was Deputy Headteacher, an opportunity to raise money for a school charity appeared in the form of a group climb of Kilimanjaro, the world's fourth highest mountain. Being a keen hiker, I signed up. The fundraising included inviting pupils to sign their name on a sheet for a sum of money so that they could say their names, if not themselves, had been on top of Africa.

Four days of enjoyable and occasionally challenging hiking with my niece in a team of 12 led us to base camp and a three-hour sleep before the final ascent starting at 10 pm. We began walking incredibly slowly. I decided to speed things up a bit, being impatient to move things forward. Mistake. Within 20 seconds my heartbeat started to race and I literally felt like my heart was about to burst through my chest. Back into line and allowing those with greater wisdom to lead and for me to relax and enjoy the journey, being part of an experienced team.

On the final ascent I had to stop to be sick. I should have turned around; however, I was determined, after having come this far, to push on. We reached the top and an apparent sunrise in a freezing fog. We ceremoniously unfurled the banner and began our descent. Half an hour later and my niece collapsed. The guides who were there immediately grabbed her, initially carrying her over their shoulders, then on a stretcher and as quickly as possible, descended. I was alone. I carried on my descent, fearful as to which way to go. However, the visibility cleared and eventually I came across and joined other members of the team. Have faith! On return to base camp, we visited the medical centre and my niece, rehydrated and smiling, was going to be fine, being fussed over by the very attentive guides. All's well that ends well.

As you draw to the end of another term, with this unique cohort of pupils and this unique team of staff, remember not to be impatient, but to use the wisdom of those around you – you are part of a wonderful team; remember not to fear – all will be well; and finally, if ever there was a time to show and inspire determination, this is it. You (and they) can do this.

 (All leaders) Evaluate key performance indicators

Securing progress by clarifying the success and growth of the school

March sees the confirmation of pupil numbers, the end of the financial year, the winning (or not) of any capital bids, and the conclusion of the options process. These provide an opportunity to reflect and possibly celebrate the continued growth and success of the school. After writing your report, use the following questions to check that you have covered these key points.

Analyse

■ Report your data on the areas/feeder schools of the pupils who are joining you and the secondary schools, universities, and employment destinations for those that are leaving.

■ How does this data compare to previous years, and the latest local and national benchmarks?

■ What positive and less positive messages about learning, teaching, and leadership come out of the recruitment and destinations of this year's pupils?

■ What patterns about learning, teaching, and leadership are there in the recruitment and destinations of this year's pupils?

Evaluate

■ What targets/goals were set to be achieved in relation to the recruitment and destinations of this year's pupils and have these targets/goals been achieved, partially achieved, or not achieved?

■ What went well and what could have been improved? Have you consulted with key staff involved in the process and enabled them to give their views in relation to the recruitment and destinations of this year's pupils?

■ What do you understand to be the reasons behind any successes and any areas that were less successful?

Action

■ What follow-up actions need to be made/key messages need to be communicated as a result of your analysis/evaluation?

■ With regard to finances, what is agreed will happen to underspend? How will this be managed?

Celebrate

Should there be good news in increased pupil numbers, successful bid applications, or a broader, more interesting range of curriculum choices, use this as a time to celebrate the way you work as a school and the success it brings. Use the following to help prepare those celebrations:

■ Arrange a method of celebrating success, giving out celebratory messages or token gifts in assembly or at a staff meeting, publishing social media posts, a press release or article for the school's newsletter/website.

- Create an opportunity to celebrate your school/department's success and make explicit the progress you are making as a school/department.

- Write letters of appreciation to key teachers and leaders for their notable positive contribution.

》》》 **(All leaders)**   **Celebrate a term well done**

Securing progress through recognising and celebrating the progress made over the spring term

---

Just before you crack open a bottle of something to celebrate the end of the spring term, there is one final job that needs to be done: Sign off the progress of the trainee and new teachers on their support programme for this term. Key questions that will help evaluate this include:

Attendance and Punctuality: Has their attendance/punctuality rate been high or dropped below expectation?

Professionalism: Have they behaved in line with the school's Code of Conduct, or have there been issues?

Teachers' Standards: Is there sufficient evidence to say they are on track to successfully meet the standards?

Evidence: Has someone checked that all the evidence that should be in place is in place?

Concerns: Are there any concerns that need addressing in the summer term?

Once all is in order, these need to be signed off and sent to the local authority/ relevant university and a celebration of the progress the trainee/new teachers have made this term should be had.

Celebrate:

- Arrange a method of celebrating success This can be through presentations or competitions, giving out prizes in assembly or at a staff meeting, publishing social media posts, or a press release or article for the school's newsletter/website.

- Create an opportunity to celebrate your school's success over the spring term and make explicit the progress you are making as a school.

- Write letters of appreciation to key teachers and leaders for their notable positive contribution.

Summary and checklist for March

LEADER ACTION	FOCUS	SENIOR LEADERS	MIDDLE LEADERS
Arrange	Begin timetable for next year		▓
	End of term and start of term arrangements		
Action	Implement mid-year Performance Appraisal Review		
	Complete end of term assessments		
	Update Coursework, Catch Up, and Revision programmes		
	Update scheme of work (SOW) for Summer 1	▓	
Analyse and applaud	Admission arrangements/Pupil recruitment		▓
	Capital bids		▓
	Options process (KS4/5)		
Action	Action end of term and start of term arrangements		

April

April is the calm before the storm, when nerves are to be steadied and positivity maintained.

April sees all the complex pieces of progress start to come together and the final picture becomes realistically clearer.

April is to be experienced with urgent pragmatism.

DOI: 10.4324/9781003129691-10

Introduction: April

April brings curriculum and assessment matters to a head. Time is at a premium as course content may still need to be taught, alongside a healthy revision programme in preparation for imminent exams. This is also the month which sees the beginning of work ahead of the new academic year. Here is what lies ahead for April.

APRIL SUMMARY		
KEY		
👍 **Action that analyses, evaluates, and celebrates previous work**	⟫ **Action that supports current work**	🕒 **Action that prepares future work**
Statutory activity (higher priority)	**Non-statutory activity (lower priority)**	
Action	*Leaders*	*School focus for April*
👍	Senior leaders	Evaluate end of term and start of term arrangements
👍	All leaders	Evaluate end of term tests
👍	Senior leaders	Evaluate Handbook/Prospectus/Job Descriptions/Calendar
⟫	All leaders	Summer monitoring and tracking in place
⟫	All leaders	Update Coursework, Catch Up, and Revision programmes
⟫	All leaders	Update website and displays
⟫	All leaders	Update school's evaluation form (SEF)/School Improvement Plan (SIP)/Faculty Improvement Plan (FIP), and continuing professional development (CPD) in light of mid-year data
🕒	Senior leaders	Prepare Annual tests and exam preparation

As April starts, create an opportunity at your next leadership team/department meeting to discuss the following standing agenda items:

- **Staffing and safeguarding**: For primary schools, April sees confirmation of Reception numbers. Are there any staffing and/or safeguarding concerns to be urgently addressed this month? (see January for staff recruitment procedures)?

- **Calendar**: Are there any pinch points this month which need to be carefully managed beforehand, especially if Easter is particularly late?

- **Trips and school activities**: Are there any trips or large group activities this month, or during the May half term, which need to be carefully managed?

- **Website and communications**: Is the website up to date and are parents/pupils/ staff clear about what is happening this month? Is there robust, challenging, and engaging online work available for pupils to complete if needed?

- **Inspection ready**: Which areas need addressing this month to ensure we are on track with our work?

The rationale for the other actions taking place this month, and in this order, include that an action is *more important* or needs doing *more urgently*, has a higher priority and therefore comes earlier in the month and vice versa. An action may be *part of a process* and so must happen before one action, but after another. Also, certain actions are *fixed* to events outside of the school's control and so these actions are tied to a particular date in the calendar (for example, external exams) or are actions *related to a fixed* event.

After the Easter break, and with so much going on, a chance to pause and reflect on the end of term and the industrious start to the summer term is essential. All end of term assessment results should be in and this as close to the real thing as it gets, so all analysis and evaluation have an urgency not generally seen elsewhere in the year. This is also the point at which preparations begin for September, and the far-reaching documents of the prospectus, staff handbook, job descriptions, and school calendar need to be reviewed as to how well they are fit for purpose and changes that need to be made are to be identified.

This leads to the main body of work in April for the school leader, monitoring and tracking progress with a last opportunity to improve coursework, catch up on previously missed work, and effectively revise previously learnt work. With so much quality content being created, April is a good opportunity to update displays, especially with word walls and mind maps to help pupils remember key information ahead of their exams/tests. Again, with a range of end of term data coming in, this is a good time for leaders to update their improvement plans and CPD programmes. Finally, if it is not underway already, the final tests/ exams that pupils need to do should now start to be considered and prepared.

 (Senior leaders)   **Celebrate the end and start of terms**

Securing progress through a continued focus on teaching, learning, and making good progress

A new term and the work continues apace. Before diving into the new term, take a moment to reflect on and confirm how well things were drawn to a close last term and how well things have settled into place this term.

Analyse

■ Report on attendance data – any issues to address/follow up?

■ How does this data compare to previous years, and the latest local and national benchmarks?

■ Have new staff/pupils arrived and how successful was their induction?

■ What positive and less than positive messages about learning, teaching, and leadership come out of the end of term/start of term?

Evaluate

■ What do you understand to be the reasons behind any successes? Can these be developed?

■ What do you understand to be the reasons behind any areas that were less successful? How are these going to be addressed and resolved?

Action

■ What follow-up actions need to be made/key messages need to be communicated as a result of your analysis/evaluation?

Celebrate

Before moving on from the start of term, spend a moment recognising and reinforcing good behaviour for learning habits that are being demonstrated across the department/school.

■ Arrange a method of celebrating a successful end to the previous term and a strong start to this term, sending out a key message through tutor time, staff briefing, or an article for the school's newsletter/website.

■ Create an opportunity to celebrate your school department's success and make explicit the progress you are making as a school/department.

■ Write letters of appreciation to key teachers and leaders for their notable positive contribution.

 (All leaders)   Celebrate the end of term results

Securing progress by recognising, publicising, and promoting pupil progress

From the end-of-spring-term tests, take a moment to consider the journey your pupils are making with you so far this year; where they started, and where they are aiming to finish. To help cross-reference how successful the test results have been over the school year, Paterson (2013), Coe (2014), and Kyriakides (2008) offer some useful insights and the Standards and Testing Agency on the Department for Education (DfE) website gives some useful guidance. More information on these can be found in Chapter 15 at the end of this book. In addition, using online tools such as Survey Monkey or Google Forms enables you to efficiently evaluate your work, saving you precious time.

After writing your report on what the data says, use the following questions to check that you have covered these key points.

Analyse

- Have you reported your data clearly and succinctly?

- What patterns have emerged related to learning and learners, teaching and teachers, and leadership and leaders?

- How does this data compare to similar data from previous years, and the latest local and national benchmarks?

- What positive and less than positive messages about learning, teaching, and leadership come out of the end of term tests of this year's pupils?

Evaluate

- What targets/goals were set to be achieved in relation to the attainment and progress of this year's pupils and have these targets/goals been achieved, partially achieved, or not achieved?

- What went well and what could have been improved? Have you consulted with key staff involved in the process and enabled them to give their views in relation to this term's end of term tests?

- What do you understand to be the reasons behind any successes and any areas that were less successful in relation to the results and reporting?

Action

- What follow-up actions need to be made/key messages need to be communicated as a result of your analysis/evaluation?

Celebrate

At the end of the spring term, this is an important milestone in each pupil's education to date. Use the following to check you have covered all the relevant bases before you send out your report on the end of term tests to the school community.

■ Reinforce aspiration. In the end of term assemblies and communications to the school community, celebrate those pupils who have achieved at or above expectations.

■ What key messages related to good practice in learning, teaching, and leadership need to be relayed and shared with the school community from the tests?

■ What behaviour for learning messages to improve practice in learning, teaching, and leadership need to be relayed and shared to the school community from the tests?

Moments that count throughout the year: Recognition

Like most Junior Schools, the school where I work as a Teaching Assistant has a weekly Celebration Assembly where individual children are recognised by their class teachers for something special – it could be anything, ranging from producing an outstanding piece of writing to showing kindness and being a good friend. All the children squash into the hall in cross-legged rows to watch the Head present the certificates, whilst the staff sit on chairs, crammed around the edge if they got in early, or perch along old-fashioned wooden gym benches if they didn't. If she's free, even the receptionist will squeeze in, such is the mood: It's a combination of Friday Feeling and anticipation.

Some years ago, this familiar weekly event took a very different turn. Our Head at the time was a much-respected, focussed, and highly professional woman. But if she was preoccupied, as she often was, she could pass you in the corridor without making eye contact or comment, and although you knew that this was because something pressing was on her mind, it could leave you feeling a bit unacknowledged. She had many strengths and qualities, but spontaneity or fun surprises were not among them, which made the events that followed during that assembly all the more astonishing …

That morning, the school community was gathered in the hall in the usual way, but instead of inviting up the children, our Head proceeded to invite the support staff up, individually, one by one, to receive a certificate. These were on the familiar templates, the same as those given each week to the children, but instead were made out to the Teaching Assistants. Thought had been given to the different areas where we personally contributed to school life, for example, mine was about art, and a colleague who was a brilliant linguist was praised for her work with EAL children. Once the certificates had all been presented and the children's applause had died down, the Head announced that the library was out of commission as she had turned it into a Nail Bar for the rest of the morning and we were to pop in and have our nails painted during a quiet moment. But before that, there was an enormous celebration cake waiting in the staff room.

At the end of that extraordinary day, as we left for the weekend with a happy glow and a set of freshly painted nails, we were all aware of having experienced "moments that count". It was quite clear to us that the emotions felt by a 28- or 48-year-old are little different from those of an eight-year-old, when it came to being clapped in assembly and presented with a certificate saying lovely things about them to stick on the fridge!

Caroline Davies, Teaching Assistant

 (Senior leaders)   Evaluate key school documents

Securing progress through having clear and comprehensive information

This is the time of year to take a thorough look at the key foundation documents of the school, ensuring they are up to date and fit for purpose. Many issues for staff and leaders (and therefore the pupils and parents) can have their roots in an out-of-date job description, handbook, or a confusing school calendar. To help cross-reference how up-to-date key documents are, The Key and Simply Docs offer some useful insights and, on their websites, give some useful guidance. More information on these can be found in Chapter 15 at the end of this book. In addition, using online tools such as Survey Monkey or Google Forms enables you to efficiently evaluate your work, saving you precious time.

Use the following questions to help your planning before taking action to improve them.

Analyse

- ▓ What feedback over the year have you received about the Staff Handbook/ Prospectus/Job Descriptions/School Calendar?

- ▓ How clear, comprehensive, and easy to understand is the relevant information for pupils/parents/staff, leaders, and Governors?

- ▓ How do the documents compare with other schools' documents/models of best practice?

Evaluate

- ▓ Consult with key staff involved in the process and enable them to give their views as to what they thought went well and what could have been improved in relation to these documents.

Action

■ What actions come out of your analysis and evaluation?

Celebrate

After analysing and evaluating your Staff Handbook/Prospectus/Job Descriptions/School Calendar, take a moment to recognise and applaud the progress you have made with them and the contribution they have made to help move the school forwards and support pupil progress.

■ Celebrate a job well done in staff meetings or through other communications to key staff and the school community, recognising the great work people are doing to help drive school improvement forward through having such high quality and important documents in good shape.

 (All leaders)   Summer monitoring and tracking in place

Securing progress by routinely checking that everyone is making expected progress

It's again that time of year that whatever our work as a leader, there will be a need to observe the areas over which you lead and report on progress. Here are some questions to help ensure your monitoring tracking is as rigorous as it needs to be:

■ Have you clearly articulated what you and others need to do, and when and where regarding monitoring and tracking of teaching and learning?

■ What are the key deadlines for the work to be completed?

■ If there are additional things for people to do, what should they do about covering their other work that is being missed?

■ What should people do if there is a problem?

Update your **file of evidence** to offer as case studies or examples of work. In addition, update your **spreadsheet**. The following are critical to any data analysis and therefore any monitoring and tracking:

■ **Target**: To what extent does current progress match the target you are aiming to achieve?

■ **Local/national benchmarks**: To what extent does current progress match the target achieved locally/nationally?

■ **Time frame**: To what extent are you on track?

- **Milestones**: To what extent have you reached those milestones you wanted to reach?

- **RAG rating**: Where in the data are things going better than expected (colour coded green), as expected (colour coded amber) and worse than expected (colour coded red) at this point in the year?

- What **follow-up actions** are needed as a result?

> **(All leaders) Review support in light of latest data**
>
> *Securing progress by not letting anyone achieve anything less than their best*

For primary schools and the SATs, and secondaries with GCSE and A-Levels imminent, with the latest round of whole school or department data coming through from the latest assessments and the Easter holidays comes an opportunity to celebrate and an opportunity to learn. Results that are at, above, and beyond what you are expecting mean the learning process, outlined below, is working very well and present a moment to celebrate and evaluate why that is – what great leadership, teaching, and learning are going on that can be shared?

However, results that are not what you are expecting means the learning process is not working as well as it could be and is an opportunity to carry out a gap analysis and urgently correct the trajectory of progress. The issue may be related to the leadership, the teaching, or the learning within the learning process. The table below illustrates some examples of this.

ISSUE	CHECK			
Inconsistent results between classes	Scheme of work	Programme of study	Assessment process	Quality of teaching
Inconsistent results for a pupil group	Prior Attainment (High/Middle/Low)	Target grades (High/Middle/Low)	Groups (special educational needs – SEN/pupil premium – PP/ English as an Additional Language – EAL)	Gender (boys/girls)
Inconsistent results for a teacher	Pitch (Difficulty)	Pace (Adaptability)	Differentiation (Accessibility)	Engagement (Style)

If from the data there are inconsistent results between teachers, consider the Education Endowment Foundation (EEF)'s guidance (2018) to see if the school needs to make improvements to the teaching and learning experience.

EDUCATION ENDOWMENT FOUNDATION'S TOP 10 RECOMMENDED SUPPORT STRATEGIES TO IMPROVE PROGRESS

Strategy	Cost	Strength of Evidence	Impact (months)
Feedback	£	✓✓✓	+8
Metacognition and self-regulation	£	✓✓✓✓	+7
Reading comprehension strategies	£	✓✓✓✓	+6
Collaborative learning	£	✓✓✓✓	+5
Oral language interventions	£	✓✓✓✓	+5
Peer tutoring	£	✓✓✓✓	+5
Mastery learning	£	✓✓✓	+5
Homework (secondary)	£	✓✓	+5
One to one tuition	££££	✓✓✓✓	+5
Phonics	£	✓✓✓✓✓	+4

When you have identified any strategies that are likely to improve school-wide practice, the next step is to look at the data for inconsistent results, or consistently poor results between pupils and any more specific patterns across the department/school.

> **Are there patterns in a particular group of pupils not achieving to the expected level?**
>
> **Meet with colleagues to discuss and agree sharing best practice through CPD and pupil intervention.**
>
> **Staff** In-Service Education and Training (**INSET**) (e.g. guidance provided at staff meeting/activities during INSET) needs to be put in place to help the team raise the quality or implement a more effective pace to teaching and learning.

If the issue is pupil related, consider the following:

ISSUE	SOLUTION	METHOD
Absence from lessons	Complete the missed work after school	Online work/Catch up programme
Inability to answer questions	Revision/exam practice/ targeted intervention	Revision groups/practice tests/ study-buddy
Insufficient work completed	Opportunities to catch up	Catch up programme/ one-to-one support/small group work

Having a strong programme of general support available to them ensures that pupils do not slip too far behind and continue to make sufficient progress. Use the upcoming Easter holidays to intensively implement these.

Last but not least, when you have identified any strategies that are likely to improve progress for key groups of pupils, the next step is to look at the inconsistent results of an individual teacher.

For each individual teacher, are there patterns in a particular group of pupils not achieving to the expected level?

Meet with colleagues to discuss and agree any necessary staff training and pupil intervention.

Focussed CPD (e.g. peer observation, team teaching, or specific training) needs to be put in place to help the team raise the quality or implement a more effective pace to teaching and learning.

For those pupils and staff underachieving for the first time, implement the actions as suggested in October. For those pupils and staff who are continuing to underachieve, implement an individual support plan as suggested in September.

 (All leaders)   **Update website and displays**

Securing progress by displaying work celebrates and makes explicit high-quality learning

---

This may seem like an additional job that is unnecessary, but to keep the working atmosphere fresh, any displays or website content that is out of date need to be removed and more up-to-date work displayed/posted. Consider the following to ensure your department/school walls continue to be interesting and stimulating:

- **Word walls** – displaying key words for pupils to incorporate into their work, conversations, and answers

- **Annotated work** – displaying exemplar work that is annotated so pupils are clear what to do to achieve a particular grade.

- **Success criteria** – Key skills are displayed with descriptors as to what needs to be accomplished to achieve successively higher grades.

- **Subject Stars** – displaying photographs of pupils and their latest grades/scores helps promote a sense of success/improvement.

Making sure any displayed work is labelled with the creator's name and tutor or year group helps promote the sense of success and achievement.

(All leaders)   Update all plans and CPD

Securing progress by checking we are achieving our targets and implementing improvements.

As we are two-thirds of the way through the year, updating the Faculty Improvement Plan, School Improvement Plan, and School Evaluation Form is important and will be the foundation for your next report to the Senior Leadership Team (SLT) or Governors in evidencing both school improvement and how inspection ready you are. Swift action to redress any issues is essential. Before completing the plans and forms, consider the following:

■ Have you clearly articulated what you and others need to do, and when and where re: updating the FIP/SIP/SEF?

■ Have you given people involved in the process an opportunity to feedback and give their views as to what they think is going well and what could be improved?

■ What is the deadline for the work to be completed?

■ What clear milestones are to be reached along the way and are they being met?

■ If the milestones are not being met, what action is being taken to redress this?

■ Have you included updating the statutory areas of Behaviour/Attendance/ SEN (including Education and Health Care Plans – EHCPs)/LAC (Looked After Children)/Behaviour Attendance/Safeguarding/Careers?

■ Have you cross-checked your actions against the latest inspection criteria and that you are Ofsted ready?

■ What should people do if there is a problem?

■ How and when are you going to follow up with the information that is recorded?

■ What leadership and teaching CPD implications arise from this update?

 (All leaders)   Arrange annual exams

Securing progress through arranging an assessment of what has been learnt over the year

In arranging the annual exams, it should be clear from the programme of study and scheme of work what learning needs to be tested. To help prepare the best exams, explore what others have written or are doing. Cooper (2017), Gill (2017), and the DfE (2016a) offer some useful insights and a number of groups, including PiXL, the DfE, and exam boards on their websites give some useful guidance.

More information on these (KS1 and 2 SATs, KS4 GCSEs, KS5 A-Levels, and BTECs) can be found in Chapter 15 at the end of this book. Also, use online tools such as Google Docs or Google Sheets to work on key documents or data concurrently with your team and ensure you work as effectively as possible. Before you start the process of arranging the end of year tests, use the following to ensure the process is as effective as it can be.

Exam preparation for teachers

In preparing pupils for their annual exams, here are 10 effective strategies that provide good value for money for teachers to ensure their pupils are exam ready.

- Peer quizzes: Pupils quiz each other on what has been learnt so far and mark/grade each other.

- Pupils revise and teacher tests previously learnt and current work, using online programmes such as Quizlet.

- Have pupils explain why an answer is right *and* why an answer is wrong.

- Use flash cards to focus pupils' minds on key terms and concepts, using online resources such as Kahoot.

- Develop exam stamina by training pupils to revise in short, intensive sessions and answer questions over longer periods of time.

- Use past papers to develop pupil exam vocabulary.

- Have pupils use Mind Maps to organise complex/detailed projects.

- Have pupils use Literacy Maps to encapsulate key terms and concepts.

- Use Spaced Retrieval in schemes of work to keep previously learnt work fresh in pupils' minds.

- Do not accept classwork or homework that is below expectation from pupils. Have them re-draft and re-submit.

Exam preparation for leaders

Similar to the preparation for the end of term assessments, in arranging the end of year exams, agree a consistent process of examinations with school leaders and the exams officer and publicise. Use the following to help prepare your end of year exams:

- Ensure all pupils have target grades given to them for each subject.

- Ensure all pupils and parents know those target grades.

- Ensure all books/files have a completed tracker sheet that has recorded results through the year.

- Consistently prepare staff and pupils for the exams, consulting and communicating agreed expectations.

- Present the process to the SLT and heads of department, so everyone is clear on the process and key deadlines.

- Discuss with the SLT/Governors as to how the process is to be quality assured and how to ensure that the information being presented is accurate and that staff are consistent in how the assessments are being carried out and data recorded.

- Set up a Question Analysis spreadsheet and discuss results at the next department meeting.

- Set up a whole school data analysis spreadsheet and discuss results at the next SLT meeting.

Summary and checklist for April

LEADER ACTION	FOCUS	SENIOR LEADERS	MIDDLE LEADERS
Analyse and applaud	End of term and start of term arrangements		
	End of term tests		
	Staff Handbook/Prospectus/Job Descriptions/School Calendar		
Action	Implement summer monitoring and tracking		
	Update Coursework, Catch Up, and Revision programmes		
	Update website and displays		
	Update SEF/SIP/FIP, and CPD in light of mid-year data		
Arrange	Annual tests/exams		

Summer term: Reaping the harvest

DOI: 10.4324/9781003129691-11

SUMMER TERM SUMMARY				
KEY				
👍 **Action that analyses, evaluates, and celebrates previous work**		≫ **Action that supports current work**	⟳ **Action that prepares future work**	
Statutory activity (higher priority)		**Non-statutory activity (lower priority)**		
A–Z of key school activities	**May**	**June**	**July**	**August**
Assemblies		👍	⟳	
Assessment programme		👍	⟳	
Budget		👍	⟳	
Census		≫		
Coursework, Catch Up, and Revision programmes	≫	👍		
End/start of term/routines / duties		⟳	⟳	
Exams and careers	≫	≫ 👍	⟳	≫
Improvement Plans			≫👍	
Induction and Summer School – external		⟳	≫	≫
Integrated framework		👍	⟳	
Leavers Year 6 in July	≫	👍		
Monitoring and tracking		👍	⟳	
Parents' Evenings		👍		
Performance appraisal and pay		👍		
Policies		👍	⟳	
Quality assurance	≫	👍		
Repairs and maintenance		⟳		≫
Routines & duties			⟳	
Schemes of Work/Personal, Social, Health, and Economic education (PSHE)	≫	👍 ⟳	≫	
Staff Handbook/Prospectus/Meetings, etc.	⟳		≫	
Staff recruitment	≫	≫ 👍	⟳	
Statutory requirements			👍	≫
Tests	≫	👍		
Timetable			≫	
Website and displays			👍 ⟳	

May

In May the die is cast. What will be will be.

May sees a whirlwind of work as teaching draws to completion, coursework and catch up is wrapped up, and revision is embedded ahead of the final assessments.

May is to be experienced with extreme tenacity.

DOI: 10.4324/9781003129691-12

Introduction: May

May sees the beginning of the end. Coursework is completed and sent off for moderation, annual tests begin and the deadline for staff resignations for the new academic year expires at the end of the month. Making sure that everything that needs to be done is done well and by the deadline is the key to May. Here is what lies ahead.

MAY SUMMARY		
KEY		
👍 Action that analyses, evaluates, and celebrates previous work	�》⟫ Action that supports current work	🕐 Action that prepares future work
Statutory activity (higher priority)	**Non-statutory activity (lower priority)**	
Action	**Leaders**	**School focus for May**
⟫⟫	All leaders	Quality Assurance – Summer programme starts
⟫⟫	All leaders	Update Coursework, Catch Up, and Revision programmes
⟫⟫	All leaders	All final coursework collected and assessed
⟫⟫	All leaders	Carry out annual exams and record/write reports
⟫⟫	Senior leaders	Implement Year 6, Year 11, or Year 13 leavers plans
⟫⟫	Senior leaders	Complete staff recruitment
⟫⟫	All leaders	Prepare Schemes of Work for Summer 2/Update Programmes of Study
🕐	All leaders	Update Handbooks/Prospectus/Job Descriptions/ School Calendar

As May starts, create an opportunity at your next leadership team/department meeting to discuss the following standing agenda items:

- ▨ **Staffing and safeguarding**: Are there any staffing and/or safeguarding concerns to be urgently addressed this month? (see January for staff recruitment procedures)?

- ▨ **Calendar**: Are there any pinch points this month which need to be carefully managed beforehand?

- **Trips and school activities**: Are there any trips or large group activities this month which need to be carefully managed?

- **Website and communications**: Is the website up to date and are parents/pupils/staff clear about what is happening this month? Is there robust, challenging, and engaging online work available for pupils to complete if needed?

- **Inspection ready**: Which areas need addressing this month to ensure we are on track with our work?

The rationale for the other actions taking place this month, and in this order, include that an action is *more important* or needs doing *more urgently*, has a higher priority and therefore comes earlier in the month and vice versa. An action may be *part of a process* and so must happen before one action, but after another. Also, certain actions are *fixed* to events outside of the school's control and so these actions are tied to a particular date in the calendar (for example, external exams) or are actions *related to a fixed* event.

The whirlwind that is May starts for leaders with a final quality assurance of work being done and a final sign off of the coursework ahead of being sent off to examiners for moderation. The process of testing and examining what pupils have learnt begins with the pupils who are leaving being given a well-organised and fond farewell. For senior leaders, there is a last-minute scramble to fill any staffing holes ahead of the May 31st resignation deadline, and an update of the final schemes of work of the year.

May also sees the point at which work begins on updating the large and important documents of the prospectus, staff, department, and trainee handbooks, job descriptions, and the school calendar; the first inkling of the preparatory work for the new academic year that lies ahead.

 (All leaders)   Summer Quality Assurance star

Securing progress by others internally or externally checking that what we do is best practice

At this point in the year, the third round of quality assurance is checking to see that what should still be in place is in place. Before taking action and quality assuring your department's, or your school's work, consider the following points to help ensure that what you continue to do is fit for purpose and effective. Having a different pair of internal eyes where there are no concerns should be sufficient. However, where concerns have continued, it is imperative that external quality assurance is used to check the quality of work taking place in the school, and either way, answer the question, is what we say in our intention being implemented? Here are a number of methods by which we can quality assure the work of the department or the school.

- Monitoring – questionnaires, observations, book looks
- Tracking – spreadsheets, data analysis, patterns
- Audits
- Displays
- Monitoring and tracking schedules
- Learning walks
- Logs
- Minutes of meetings
- Observations and feedback
- Other quality assurance (internal)
- Other quality assurance (external)

Use these to provide evidence that the methods by which leaders lead, teachers teach, and pupils learn are optimal. Where learning, teaching, and leadership is sub-optimal, this needs to be identified, reported, and supported with the sharing of best practice and a plan of action. This is important as it will provide the evidence should subsequent results be below expectation.

There should be no surprises in the results because the quality assurance programme is effective and fit for purpose. See September for more details.

 (All leaders)   Review support in light of latest data

Securing progress by not letting anyone achieve anything less than their best

For primary schools and the SATs, and secondaries with GCSE and A-Levels imminent, and with the last round of whole school or department data coming through from the latest assessments comes an opportunity to celebrate and an opportunity to learn. Results that are at, above, and beyond what you are expecting means the learning process, outlined below, is working very well and present a moment to celebrate and evaluate why that is – what great leadership, teaching, and learning is going on that can be shared?

Leadership | Teaching | Learning | Results

However, results that are not what you are expecting means the learning process is not working as well as it could be and is an opportunity to carry out a gap analysis and urgently correct the trajectory of progress. The issue may be related to the leadership, the teaching, or the learning within the learning process. The table below illustrates some examples of this.

ISSUE	CHECK			
Inconsistent results between classes	Scheme of work	Programme of study	Assessment process	Quality of teaching
Inconsistent results for a pupil group	Prior attainment (High/Middle/Low)	Target grades (High/Middle/Low)	Groups (special educational needs – SEN/pupil premium – PP/ English as an Additional Language – EAL)	Gender (boys/girls)
Inconsistent results for a teacher	Pitch (Difficulty)	Pace (Adaptability)	Differentiation (Accessibility)	Engagement (Style)

If from the data there are inconsistent results between teachers, consider the Education Endowment Foundation (EEF)'s guidance (2018) to see if the school needs to make improvements to the teaching and learning experience.

EDUCATION ENDOWMENT FOUNDATION'S TOP 10 RECOMMENDED SUPPORT STRATEGIES TO IMPROVE PROGRESS

Strategy	Cost	Strength of evidence	Impact (months)
Feedback	£	✓✓✓	+8
Metacognition and self-regulation	£	✓✓✓✓	+7
Reading comprehension strategies	£	✓✓✓✓	+6
Collaborative learning	£	✓✓✓✓	+5
Oral language interventions	£	✓✓✓✓	+5
Peer tutoring	£	✓✓✓✓	+5
Mastery learning	£	✓✓✓	+5
Homework (secondary)	£	✓✓	+5
One to one tuition	££££	✓✓✓✓	+5
Phonics	£	✓✓✓✓✓	+4

When you have identified any strategies that are likely to improve school-wide practice, the next step is to look at the data for inconsistent results, or consistently poor results between pupils and any more specific patterns across the department/ school.

> Are there patterns in a particular group of pupils not achieving to the expected level?
>
> Meet with colleagues to discuss and agree sharing best practice through continuing professional development (CPD) and pupil intervention.
>
> Staff INSET (e.g. guidance provided at staff meeting/activities during In-Service Education and Training (INSET) needs to be put in place to help the team raise the quality or implement a more effective pace to teaching and learning.

If the issue is pupil related, consider the following:

ISSUE	SOLUTION	METHOD
Absence from lessons	Complete the missed work after school	Online work/Catch up programme
Inability to answer questions	Revision/exam practice/ targeted intervention	Revision groups/practice tests/ study-buddy
Insufficient work completed	Opportunities to catch up	Catch up programme/one-to-one support/small group work

Having a strong programme of general support available to them ensures that pupils do not slip too far behind and continue to make sufficient progress.

Last but not least, when you have identified any strategies that are likely to improve progress for key groups of pupils, the next step is to look at the inconsistent results of an individual teacher.

> For each individual teacher, are there patterns in a particular group of pupils not achieving to the expected level?
>
> Meet with colleagues to discuss and agree any necessary staff training and pupil intervention.
>
> Focused CPD (e.g. peer observation, team teaching, or specific training) needs to be put in place to help the team raise the quality or implement a more effective pace to teaching and learning.

For those pupils and staff underachieving for the first time, implement the actions as suggested in October. For those pupils and staff who are continuing to underachieve, implement an individual support plan as suggested in September.

(All leaders)   All final coursework assessed

Securing progress by not letting anyone achieve anything less than their best

Before you embark on the final push to collect in all coursework, use the following to help check that you have covered all the actions that are needed are done to ensure the best possible grades for the pupils.

▧ Are all the resources needed to do the work in place?

▧ Is everyone sufficiently skilled to do the work you want them to do?

> **If the answer is no to the above, consider delaying the start of the work until there are sufficient resources/staff are sufficiently trained and skilled in what to do**

▧ Be clear in articulating what you and others need to do and how to do it.

▧ Be clear in articulating how staff/pupils' work will benefit as a result of what you are doing.

▧ Set a clear deadline for the work to be completed.

▧ Set clear milestones to be reached along the way.

▧ Model what success looks like. To what extent is best practice being shared, e.g. in staff INSET/CPD?

▧ Be clear about what people should do if there is a problem.

 (All leaders)   Annual exams begin / reports written

Securing progress through recognising and reporting pupil progress in their assessments

To ensure every pupil is included and receives the results from their annual tests, use the following to check the process you have in place is robust and comprehensive.

▧ All pupils have received their latest grades.

▧ All parents have received an update and have been given their child's latest grades.

- All books/files/tracker sheets/pupil records have been updated.

- A question analysis is underway by departments and put on has been put on the agenda for the next department meeting.

- Whole school data analysis is underway by the Senior Leadership Team (SLT) and has been put on the agenda for the next SLT meeting.

- SLT are following up to ensure all tests have been completed, all results have been recorded, and all reports have been written.

- SLT/Governors are quality assuring that the information being presented is accurate and that staff are consistent in how the assessments are being carried out, results are being recorded, and reports are being written.

Useful websites and more information on these (KS1 and 2 SATs, KS4 GCSEs, and KS5 A-Levels and BTECs) can be found in Chapter 15 at the end of this book.

 (Senior leaders)   Confirm and implement leavers plans

Securing progress by having clear, ambitious goals for our pupils

---

And here we are. For Year 6, Year 11, and Year 13, the end of an era and the door to the next stage of their career is within touching distance. Attention must now be turned to ensuring the school effectively supports the pupils in their transition to the next stage of their education, employment, or training with the best send-off they can have. From the plans you put in place in January, it is now time to put those plans into action. See June's Prize Giving checklist to help prepare any celebrations. In addition, here are some pointers to help you celebrate and give the most senior pupils in their key stage the best send-off you can.

- Is there a clear schedule/plan of action in place to ensure the school leavers' celebrations go as smoothly and successfully as they can?

- Have you clearly articulated what you, staff, parents, and pupils need to do, and when and where regarding school leavers celebrations?

- What is the deadline for each group to confirm their attendance/involvement with the celebrations?

- What should people do if there is a problem?

Moments that count in May: Leaving school – a rite of passage

Leaving school is a rite of passage. For long-serving teachers, it can be the case that after a while, one Year 6, Year 11, or Year 13 group blends into another. But this masks the reality of the situation; this cusp, this moment, is the pupils' moment, not the teachers. For the pupils, this is their only chance at being in Year 6, Year 11, or Year 13 before flying the nest to bigger and greater things. Facilitating their departure and celebrating with them their unique journey in their own style is the role of the school leader at this moment that counts.

Year 11 leavers assembly example speech: To Growing Up

I'm going to start a campaign, a new movement, a new political party.
It's called "Back to my childhood", "Back to my school days", "Back to the good old days".
And these are my manifesto pledges:
Get rid of mobile phones, iPads, iPods, iPuds and anything else I!
Get rid of Sky! Get rid of Computer games! Get rid of Apps and all social media!
Instead, bring back typewriters, bring back black boards, bring back mutton pie.
Bring back sago, bring back chalk, bring back Woolworths!
Bring back Captain Pugwash, Top Cat, Scooby Doo, and The Clangers!
Ah – But we can't. What is done cannot be undone.
And what is done cannot be undone. Whether we want to or not.
What we do know is that things will change.
Usually change for the better and sometimes change for the worse.
But either way – things will change.
And that brings me to this moment. This here and now. This final assembly.
So, this is the end. The last time we come together as a year group.
And what has come together over the years must now come apart.
You are moving silently and imperceptibly from must, to could.
To choice, to responsibility, to freedom.
To growing up.
So – You're going to start a campaign, a new movement, a new political party.
It's called "Into the future", It's called "Into adulthood",
It's called "You".

(All leaders)   **Update staff recruitment for September**

Securing progress by ensuring continuous, high-quality teaching, and learning

With the May 31st deadline looming, it will be increasingly clear as to the permanent staffing that will be in place in September. Any changes to this need to be filled as soon as possible to avoid the need for supply or job sharing in the new term. This can be very time-consuming. As well as the staff recruitment checklist from January, use the following to support your work in replacing much-needed staff:

■ Confirm resignations with effect from 31st May.

■ Consult and liaise with relevant staff over any deletions/amendments to existing/creation of new roles.

■ Amend job descriptions as required.

■ Identify and liaise with any internal candidates that may be suitable for the new role.

■ Advertise for the new role as soon as possible.

■ Interview and secure staffing for all roles in September.

 (Middle leaders) – Update Schemes of Work for Summer 2

Securing progress by providing a comprehensive, clear, and achievable curriculum

To help prepare the best schemes of work, explore what others have written or are doing. Ofsted (2017) and Harpham (2020) offer some useful insights and The Key, exam boards, or the TES on their websites give some useful guidance. More information on these can be found in Chapter 15 at the end of this book. Also, use online tools such as Google Docs or Google Sheets to work on key documents or data concurrently with your team and ensure you work as effectively as possible. As you review/prepare your scheme of work for the end of the summer term, use the following to check it is as good as it can be:

■ Are the **aims** of the scheme of work and each lesson **realistically high**, **clearly articulated**, and **ordered coherently** so progress over the scheme of work is **explicit**?

■ Is the work to be completed **manageable**, **challenging**, and **consistently focused on pupil learning**?

■ Is there explicit **progression in understanding** from description and facts to analysis and reasoning?

▓ Is there a clear **increase in the challenge/complexity of knowledge and skills** being learnt?

▓ Is the work expected to be completed **increasingly longer and harder**?

▓ Are activities progressing **from the class/group** to the **individual** over time and do they **include homework**?

▓ Is the **assessment for learning built into each lesson** and does it move **from informal to formal assessment**?

▓ What **provisions are in place** should anyone fall behind, or finish sooner than expected?

This is also the time to start reviewing and updating your longer-term plan or programme of study. The programme of study ensures that the curriculum has **pace**, is **structured**, and is **consistently experienced** across the school; as a result, the curriculum will **support the faster progress** of the pupils and empower and create more **confident** learners as a result. There are a number of websites that can support this, including the Department for Education (DfE) who have comprehensive content for each subject and Key Stage's programme of study, but also templates, especially for primary schools.

When writing a programme of study, it should be **clear**, **comprehensive, and coherent**:

Clear

▓ The **outcome** for each topic/scheme of work is clear.
▓ The **content and timing** for each topic are clear.
▓ The **skills and knowledge** being developed are clear.
▓ **Homework** and **assessment** opportunities are clear.

Comprehensive
▓ **All the curriculum** that is required **by law and the exam boards** to be taught is included.

Coherent
▓ **Each topic supports subsequent topics** in each programme of study.

Use the following ahead of any communications to help inform the update of the schemes of work and long-term plans, so they are as good as they can be for the new school year.

▓ Have "Schemes of work and long-term plans" as an agenda item and get as many views as is reasonable to ensure you get a strong understanding of what needs to be done to have a smooth start to the year and effective routines in place next term.

■ Identify and agree any work to be done.

■ Save time: Use last year's information/guidance that went out and amend it to what you need.

■ Propose the best: Provide a proposal that incorporates research and shares best practice in what you do, e.g. in staff INSET/CPD.

■ Propose the most workable solution: Pilot your proposal with a few trusted colleagues to give you feedback on your proposal. This will ensure that your proposal is as successful as it can be.

■ Keep it flexible: Once your proposal is live, welcome feedback on what is going well and how it could be improved further. Review and tweak accordingly. Put out the final version when ready.

Overleaf is a template for use in either primary or secondary schools. An electronic copy of this long-term plan /programme of study checklist can be found and downloaded from the School Leader's Resources page at: www.schoolleaderdev elopment.com.

PROGRAMME OF STUDY/LONG-TERM PLAN TEMPLATE						
Week	Dates	Week A/B	Lesson	Specification content	Unit/topic/paper	Homework tasks
0		No teaching				
1		A	1			
			2			
			3			
2		B	1			
			2			
			3			
			4			
3		A	1			
			2			
			3			
4		B	1			
			2			
			3			
			4			
5		A	1			
			2			
			3			
6		B	1			
			2			
			3			
			4			
7		A	1			
			2			
			3			
Half term break						

(All leaders)   **Update all key documents**

Securing progress by having comprehensive foundations that promote pupil welfare and success

---

To help prepare the best school documents, explore what others have written or are doing. The Key and Simply Docs offer some useful insights, and their website gives some useful guidance. More information on these can be found in Chapter 15 at the end of this book. Also, use online tools such as Google Docs or Google Sheets to work on key documents or data concurrently with your team and ensure you work as effectively as possible.

After reviewing and evaluating the staff handbook, departmental handbooks, trainee teacher handbooks, the prospectus, job descriptions, school calendar, and meetings schedule, it should be clear what needs to be kept and what needs changing. Before you start the process, especially where significant updates are necessary, use the following to ensure the process is as effective as it can be.

- Have "Handbooks, Prospectus, Job descriptions, School Calendar and meetings schedule", as an agenda item and get as many views as is reasonable to ensure you get a strong understanding of what needs to be updated.

- Save time: Get copies/model examples of what you want and amend them to what you need.

- Propose the best: Provide a proposal that incorporates research and shares best practice in what you do, e.g. in staff INSET/CPD.

- Propose the most workable solution: Pilot your proposal with a few trusted colleagues to give you feedback on your proposal. This will ensure that your proposal is as successful as it can be.

- Keep it flexible: Once your proposal is live, welcome feedback on what is going well and how it could be improved further. Review and tweak accordingly. Put out the final version when ready.

Summary and checklist for May

LEADER ACTION	FOCUS	SENIOR LEADERS	MIDDLE LEADERS
Action	Quality assurance – summer programme starts		
	Update Catch Up programme		
	All final coursework collected and assessed		
	Carry out annual exams and write reports		
	Implement Year 6, Year 11, or Year 13 leavers plans		
	Complete staff recruitment		
	Update scheme of work (SOW) for Summer 2		
Arrange	Update Handbooks/Prospectus/Job Descriptions/School Calendar		

June

June is the month of the academic harvest.

As the most important exams in a pupil's lifetime are experienced, the school's work over the year is weighed in the balance for its effectiveness.

June is a month to be experienced with individual and collective reflection and constructive clarity.

DOI: 10.4324/9781003129691-13

Introduction: June

With the exam season in full swing, leader attention during June can be turned to other matters. This includes ensuring a smooth transition from one year to the next, carrying forward all best practice, and having a deep reflection on the previous year, identifying any improvements that need to be made ahead of September. Here is what you have in store for June.

JUNE SUMMARY		
KEY		
👍 **Action that analyses, evaluates, and celebrates previous work**	≫ **Action that supports current work**	☾ **Action that prepares future work**
Statutory activity (higher priority)		**Non-statutory activity (lower priority)**
Action	**Leaders**	**School focus for June**
≫	All leaders	Complete annual exams and write reports
≫	All leaders	Complete and return the summer term census
≫	Senior leaders	Complete last-minute staff recruitment
☾	All leaders	Prepare Staff/Pupil Induction and Summer School
☾	All leaders	Prepare duties/routines/end of summer/start of autumn terms arrangements
☾	Senior leaders	Prepare the summer Repairs and Maintenance programme
👍☾	All leaders	Evaluate Schemes of Work, Personal, Social, Health and Economic education (PSHE), and Programmes of Study
👍	All leaders	Evaluate Assessment programme
👍	All leaders	Evaluate Coursework, Catch Up, and Revision programme
👍	All leaders	Evaluate Monitoring and Tracking programme
👍	All leaders	Evaluate the internal and external quality assurance programme
👍	All leaders	Evaluate Assemblies and Inspiring Minds programme
👍	Senior leaders	Evaluate Year 6, 11, and 13 leavers procedures
👍	Senior leaders	Evaluate Parents' Evenings
👍	All leaders	Evaluate School Policies
👍	All leaders	Evaluate staff recruitment and retention
👍	All leaders	Evaluate the budget and the integrated work of the school
👍	All leaders	Evaluate the Performance Appraisal process
👍	All leaders	Evaluate tests, exams, the careers programme, and reports

As June begins, create an opportunity at your next leadership team/department meeting to discuss the following standing agenda items:

- **Staffing and Safeguarding**: Are there any staffing and/or safeguarding concerns to be urgently addressed this month (see January for staff recruitment procedures)?

- **Calendar**: Are there any pinch points this month which need to be carefully managed beforehand?

- **Trips and school activities**: Are there any trips or large group activities this month which need to be carefully managed?

- **Website and communications**: Is the website up to date and are parents/pupils/ staff clear about what is happening this month? Is there robust, challenging, and engaging online work available for pupils to complete if needed?

- **Inspection ready**: Which areas need addressing this month to ensure we are on track with our work?

The rationale for the other actions taking place this month, and in this order, include that an action is *more important* or needs doing *more urgently*, has a higher priority and therefore comes earlier in the month and vice versa. An action may be *part of a process* and so must happen before one action, but after another. Also, certain actions are *fixed* to events outside of the school's control and so these actions are tied to a particular date in the calendar (for example, external exams), or are actions *related to a fixed* event.

Deep breath! June sees a mammoth amount of work to do, and if you are not careful, this could lead to corners being cut. However, in June, you have time. Be organised and get the work done! As pupils continue to complete their annual exams and staff are engrossed in marking, feedback, and writing reports, June is the month where school leaders can lift their eyes from the immediate, review the annual work of the school, and ensure the road ahead into the new school year is a smooth one. Last month may have seen some last-minute resignations that need to be filled urgently. This is a top priority at this stage. Other important things to consider here are all related to the summer holidays. These include pupil/staff induction and Summer School, the end of term/start of term arrangements, and the major programme of repairs and maintenance through the summer holidays.

Once the end of year tests have been completed and the year is starting to draw to a close, this is the month to do a major review of the key processes and procedures of the school, so that any improvements to be made can be put into place ahead of the summer holidays. These include schemes of work and programmes of study; the assessment programme; coursework, catch up, and revision programmes; the monitoring and tracking programme; the internal and external quality assurance programme; assemblies and the Inspiring Minds Programme; Year 6, 11, and 13 leavers procedures; parents' evenings; school policies; staff recruitment and retention; the school budget and integrated framework; the performance appraisal process and tests, the annual exams, and reports. Here is what lies ahead in June to support you in a little more detail.

 (All leaders)   Annual exams end / reports distributed
Securing progress through recognising and reporting pupil progress in their assessments

To ensure every pupil is included and receives the results from their annual tests, use the following to check the process you have in place is robust and comprehensive.

■ All pupils have received their latest grades.

■ All parents have received an update and been given their child's latest grades.

■ All books/files/tracker sheets and pupil records have been updated.

■ A question analysis is underway by departments and has been put on the agenda for the next department meeting.

■ Whole school data analysis is underway by the Senior Leadership Team (SLT) and has been put on the agenda for next SLT meeting.

■ Head of Sixth form is ensuring Year 12's have updated their personal statements and begun their post-18 employment/university/training preparation programme.

■ SLT are following up to ensure all tests have been completed, all results have been recorded, and all reports have been written.

■ SLT/Governors are quality assuring that the information being presented is accurate and that staff are consistent in how the assessments are being carried out, results are being recorded, and reports are written.

 (All leaders)   Complete summer term census
Securing progress by ensuring everyone has the most up-to-date information on pupils

Having (successfully!) run this process in October and February, everything should be in place for a smooth, efficient data gathering process this month. Ahead of actioning work on the census, spend a short time checking the groundwork is prepared and the process will run like clockwork:

■ Consult the latest guidance on the Census for any updates/changes (see Chapter 15 for useful websites).

■ Is everyone involved at the various stages prepared and ready?

■ Are you clear and have you communicated to relevant staff what needs to happen, and by when and by whom?

■ What are the biggest challenges that lie ahead and how are those challenges going to be met?

■ From the data, what are the key messages that need to be communicated to staff, leaders, and Governors?

■ Keep it flexible: Once your proposal is live, welcome feedback on what is going well and how it could be improved further.

 (Senior leaders)   Complete all staff recruitment for September

Securing progress by ensuring continuous, high-quality teaching and learning

With the May 31st deadline in the past, it may be necessary to recruit permanent staff for September. Any changes to this need to be filled as soon as possible to avoid the need for supply or job sharing in the new term. In addition to the staff recruitment checklist (see January), use the following to support your urgent work to replace staff that are leaving:

■ Confirm resignations with effect from 31 May.

■ Consult and liaise with relevant staff over any deletions/amendments to existing/creation of new roles.

■ Amend job descriptions as required.

■ Identify and liaise with any internal candidates that may be suitable for the new role.

■ Advertise for the new role as soon as possible.

■ Interview and secure staffing for all roles in September.

Moments that count in June: Recognising progress

January 2008 I was appointed substantive Headteacher in a two-form entry primary school. In September 2007, the school opened against the wish of parents and members of the local community who fought for more than a year to stop the process. It was my biggest challenge yet, with significant underachievement across the school, staff new to teaching in year groups, and a poor building unfit for purpose. However, it was the introduction of mark making in all year groups that secured a shift from poor behaviour to concentration and a belief they the pupils could achieve. Mark making was timetabled every day for 10 minutes and integrated into their topic work. There is potential in every child and this gave them a tool to improve their concentration; there was no marking just sharing verbally the marks they were doing. The pride they had in their work was unbelievable improving their presentation and language as they developed their descriptive vocabulary and ability to look at objects and the environment in detail. I was so proud of them and during our second Ofsted, the first of which was within seven weeks of being appointed, the children articulated their work effectively, something they had previously found difficult.

It was a miracle seeing the children blossom and with eyes on our school and on how we're going to improve the quality of provision; this was one of the strategies. I wanted the community to refocus and stop the constant negativism about the school. We held an art exhibition with a buffet as their love for art flourished with the enthusiasm and direction of teaching assistants who were creative. It was a major success. I was asked to share how I implemented mark making and its impact in the school at a Headteachers conference. I decided to take some of my pupils; they were up for it. I bought a fish for each group of Headteachers as the stimulus. The children's eyes lit up at the reaction of the Headteachers looking at this smelly fish, just what we wanted; a conversation, a description of the smell, and how it made them feel. The group of children went into action, questioning the Headteachers to describe the fish not only by its smell and to look closer at the lines, its gill, its eyes. There are some things you have to see for yourself and this was one of those, a memorable moment. The best was yet to come when the Headteachers questioned the children why they liked mark making. The response was it makes me happy you feel you have achieved instead of failing. It stops me from talking, I am too busy thinking of the marks and it calms the class. One went on to say It helps behaviour when everyone else concentrates. I feel calm, like I am all alone. Remarkably one of our boys walked closer towards the Heads sitting behind their desk and said with arms stretched and touching the table I don't just look at this table anymore; it's not just a table look closer. I just stood there in amazement the Moment that counts, and where did he find such confidence? Look at the lines in the wood shades of colour any sceptics questioning its validity could not argue against this. This child who previously struggled had confirmed my presentation on the benefits to the child and to the school.

At the end of the workshop one of the Headteachers said, I wasn't sure about attending your workshop, thinking how it will change behaviour and improve concentration. Thank you because I believe in what you have just shared with your children. I work in a similar challenging school and have decided to introduce this. To top its success, one of the pupils had their mark making and written work published in NAPE (National Association of Primary Education) and became a writer stimulated and motivated by Mark Making.

Yvonne Davis, Headteacher

 (All leaders)   Arrange inductions and Summer School

Securing progress by getting everyone into good working/learning habits right from the start

To help prepare the best induction programme and Summer School with the relevant staff involved, explore what others have written or are doing. The Department for Education (2018b) offer some useful insights and The Key on their website gives some useful guidance. More information on these can be found in Chapter 15 at the end of this book. Also, use online tools such as Google Docs or Google Sheets to work on key documents or data concurrently with your team and ensure you work as effectively as possible.

Before you start the process of arranging staff and pupil induction and the Summer School, use the following to help get your thoughts in order and the information you need to complete a successful project:

■ Consult: Get as many views as is reasonable (10% minimum) to ensure you get a strong understanding of what the school does well and issues that need addressing regarding induction and Summer School.

■ Save time: Get copies/model examples of what you want and amend them to what you need.

■ Propose the best: Provide a proposal that incorporates research and shares best practice in what you do, e.g. in staff In-Service Education and Training (INSET)/continuing professional development (CPD).

■ Propose the most workable solution: Pilot your proposal with a few trusted colleagues to give you feedback on your proposal. This will ensure that your proposal is as successful as it can be.

■ Keep it flexible: Once your proposal is live, welcome feedback on what is going well and how it could be improved further. Review and tweak accordingly.

Just before you send out the final schedule and plan of action, use the following to check you have covered all key points:

■ Are you clear and have you communicated to relevant staff what needs to happen, and by when and by whom?

■ Have you covered any key challenges that lie ahead and how those challenges are going to be addressed?

 (Senior leaders) **Prepare routines / end and start of terms**

Securing progress through a continued focus on teaching, learning, and making good progress

We're considering the end of the year already?! The end of the summer term, post-exams, can be a time when teaching and learning can become frayed and unfocused and as a result, leadership is completely responsive to events rather than directing and leading them. Use the following ahead of any communications to help inform the review of duties, routines, and rooming, and the end of term and Prize Giving/start of term arrangements to help keep them focused and positive.

■ Have "Duties", "Rooming", "Routines", "Prize Giving", and "End of Summer Term/Start of Autumn Term" as agenda items and get as many views as is reasonable to ensure you get a strong understanding of what needs to be done to improve the running of the school, celebrate pupil success, and to wrap up the term. Specify any work to be done over the summer holidays and start the next term.

■ Save time: Use last year's information/guidance that went out and amend it to what you need (see September for a list of the different duties/school routines to be considered).

■ Co-ordinate: Check what other schools are doing and if applicable, align your holidays with theirs.

■ Propose the best: Provide a proposal that incorporates research and shares best practice in what you do, e.g. in staff INSET/CPD.

■ Propose the most workable solution: Pilot your proposal with a few trusted colleagues to give you feedback on your proposal. This will ensure that your proposal is as successful as it can be.

■ Keep it flexible: Once your proposal is live, welcome feedback on what is going well and how it could be improved further. Review and tweak accordingly. Put out the final version when ready.

Below is a template for use in either primary or secondary schools. An electronic copy of this prize giving checklist can be found and downloaded from the School Leader's Resources page at: www.schoolleaderdevelopment.com.

ACTION	TIMING	STAFF
Venue, date, and time decided and on school calendar	1 year before	
Venue booked	1 year before	
Guest speaker arranged	6 months before	
Prize-winners nominated	6 weeks before	
Invitations sent out	5 weeks before	
PTA asked to organise refreshments	4 weeks before	
Photographer booked	4 weeks before	
Trophies engraved/polished	4 weeks before	
Order of evening decided and printed	4 weeks before	
Prize-winners notified	4 weeks before	
Music delegated	4 weeks before	
RSVPs received	2 weeks before	
Prizes bought	2 weeks before	
Readers/speakers/vote of thanks briefed	2 weeks before	
Prize-winners' seating plan decided	1 week before	
PA system and staging organised	1 week before	
Site team briefed	1 week before	
Floral arrangements sourced	1 week before	
Head teacher's speech written	1 week before	
Venue set up	Night before	
Dress rehearsal with prize-winners	On the day	
Prize Giving		
Press release sent	Day after	
Thank you letters written and sent	Day after	
Planning notes filed for next year	Day after	
Collection of trophies arranged	Day after	

 (Senior leaders) Arrange summer repairs programme

An improved working environment increases the chances of pupils achieving success

To help prepare the best repairs and maintenance programme, explore what others have written or are doing. The Department for Education – DfE (2016b) offers some useful insights and your Local Education Authority will be able to give some useful guidance. More information on these can be found in Chapter 15 at the end of this book. Also, use online tools such as Google Docs or Google Sheets to work on key documents or data concurrently with your team and ensure you work as effectively as possible.

- Have "Summer Repairs and maintenance programme" as an agenda item and get as many views as is reasonable to ensure you get a strong understanding of what needs to be done over the summer holidays.

- If needed, prioritise which work is more **important** (statutory, currently breaching health and safety, or safeguarding), or more **urgent** (high risk of injury or accident).

- Where other decisions need to be made, consider **cost** (the cheaper option may be better, but not necessarily) and **impact** (which items will help improve the learning environment and have the most impact on learning?).

- Propose the most workable solution: Pilot your proposal with a few trusted colleagues to give you feedback on your proposal. This will ensure that your proposal is as successful as it can be.

- Keep it flexible: Once your proposal is live, welcome feedback on what is going well and how it could be improved further. Review and tweak accordingly. Put out the final version when ready.

As the academic year draws to a close, take a moment to evaluate and celebrate a number of key school activities. I have presented each of the activities and some related documents and websites in the table below. To help cross-reference how successful they have been over the school year, refer to what others have written or published on websites that either confirm that what you are doing is best practice, or offer guidance as to how the school's practice might be improved. More information on these can be found in Chapter 15 at the end of this book. In addition, using online tools such as Survey Monkey or Google Forms enables you to efficiently evaluate your work, saving you precious time.

For each of the activities in the table below, use the bullet points after the table under "analyse", "evaluate", "action", and "celebrate" to ensure that you have covered these key points in any reports or communications.

LEADERS	EVALUATE AND CELEBRATE	KEY DOCUMENTS	WEBSITES
All	Schemes of Work, PSHE, and Programmes of Study	Ofsted (2017) and Harpham (2020)	The Key, TES, and exam boards
All	Assessment programme	Christodoulou (2016) and Wiliam (2018)	DfE, the Education Endowment Foundation (EEF), and PiXL
All	Coursework, Catch Up, and Revision programmes	Hanson (2004) and Coates (2015)	PiXL and the EEF
All	Monitoring and Tracking programme	Nasen (2014) and McCluskey (2017)	EEF and Pupil Progress

LEADERS	EVALUATE AND CELEBRATE 	KEY DOCUMENTS	WEBSITES
All	Internal and external quality assurance programme	Bubb and Earley (2009) and the EC (2018)	Ofsted
All	Assemblies and Inspiring Minds programme	The DfE (1994) and Foster (2018)	BBC and TES
Senior	Year 6, Year 11, and Year 13 leavers programmes	N/A	DfE, Twinkl, Teachwire
All	Parents' Evenings	N/A	SIMS, GroupCall, and ParentMail
All	School Policies	DfE (2014c) and Law (2000)	DfE and Hub4Leaders
All	Staff recruitment and retention processes	The DfE (2019a)	DfE and the Key
All	The budget and the integrated work of the school	Reynolds (2014)	DfE
All	Performance appraisal process	DfE (2019b, 2019c, and 2019e)	DfE and The Key
All	Pupil performance in exams and tests	Gill (2017) and Cooper (2017)	DfE and exam boards

Analyse

▓ What went well and what has not gone as well as hoped over the year with regard to each of the above activities?

▓ How does this compare to previous years?

▓ What positive messages/patterns about learning, teaching, and leadership come out of each of the above activities this year?

▓ What areas/patterns for improvement in learning, teaching, and leadership come out of each of the above activities?

Evaluate

▓ What targets/goals were set and to what extent have they been achieved, partially achieved, or not achieved?

▓ What went well and what could have been improved? Have you consulted with key staff involved in the process and enabled them to give their views?

▓ What are the reasons behind any successes and any areas that were less successful?

Action

- What follow-up actions related to learning, teaching, and leadership need to be made, or key messages communicated as a result of your analysis/evaluation?

Celebrate

- Celebrate: Arrange a method of celebrating success, whether this is through sharing or presenting examples of good practice or sending letters of appreciation to key teachers and leaders for their notable positive contribution.

- Ensure there is an updated file with all current work available to the respective teams, so the work completed over the year is banked and can be developed and improved in future years.

Summary and checklist for June

LEADER ACTION	FOCUS	SENIOR LEADERS	MIDDLE LEADERS
Action	Complete annual exams and recording/writing reports		
	Complete and return the summer term census		▓
	Complete last-minute staff recruitment		
Arrange	Staff/pupil Induction and Summer School		
	Prize Giving and end of term/start of term arrangements		▓
	The summer Repairs and Maintenance programme		▓
Analyse and Applaud	Schemes of Work and Programmes of Study		
	Assessment programme		
	Coursework, Catch Up, and Revision programmes		
	Monitoring and Tracking programme		
	The internal and external quality assurance programme		
	Assemblies and Inspiring Minds programme		▓
	Year 6, 11, and 13 leavers procedures		▓
	Parents' Evenings		
	School Policies		
	Staff recruitment and retention		
	The integrated work of the school		
	The Performance Appraisal process		
	Annual exams and reports		

July

For the school leader, July is a month of high pressure in successfully drawing one year to a close and having everything improved and prepared for the next.

However, it is also the month when the pressure valve can finally be released, and we fully appreciate the welcome summer holidays.

DOI: 10.4324/9781003129691-14

Introduction: July

With only three weeks available to get the required work done, and with the amount of work to be done similar to what was done in June, July is highly pressured. Much needs to be updated and put to bed before the summer holidays begin. Here is what you have in store for July.

JULY SUMMARY		
KEY		
👍 **Action that analyses, evaluates, & celebrates previous work**	》》 **Action that supports current work**	🕑 **Action that prepares future work**
Statutory activity (higher priority)	**Non-statutory activity (lower priority)**	
Action	*Leaders*	*School focus for July*
👍	All leaders	Evaluate all statutory requirements
👍 🕑	Senior leaders	Evaluate and confirm updates to the school environment/display areas
》》 👍	All leaders	Final update of Improvement Plans Faculty Improvement Plan (FIP)/ School Evaluation Form(SIP)/ School Evaluation Form(SEF)/CPD
🕑	Senior leaders	Prepare celebration of exam results and careers options
🕑	All leaders	Prepare the start of the autumn term/routines/duties
》》	All leaders	Prepare Schemes of Work for Autumn term 1
🕑	All leaders	Update Assessment programme
🕑	All leaders	Update monitoring and tracking programme
🕑	Senior leaders	Update School Policies
🕑	Senior leaders	Update Assemblies and Inspiring Minds Programme
👍 🕑	All leaders	Review and arrange Open Evening and Open Week
🕑	Senior leaders	Update staff recruitment process and procedures
🕑	Senior leaders	Update the budget and the integrated work of the school
》》	All leaders	Deliver pupil and staff induction and begin Summer School
》》	Senior leaders	Distribute Timetable/Handbook/Prospectus/Job Descriptions
》》	All leaders	Implement Prize Giving and end of term arrangements

As July starts, create an opportunity at your next leadership team/department meeting to discuss the following standing agenda items:

■ **Staffing and safeguarding**: Are there any outstanding staff and/or safeguarding concerns to be urgently addressed this month (e.g. staffing, induction, performance appraisal reviews)?

■ **Calendar**: Are there any pinch points this month which need to be carefully managed beforehand?

■ **Trips and school activities**: Are there any trips or large group activities this month which need to be carefully managed (especially the last week of term and end of year celebrations)?

■ **Website and communications**: Is the website up to date and are parents/pupils/staff clear about what is happening this month (especially regarding tidying up rooms and offices before the holidays start)?

■ **Inspection ready**: Which areas need addressing this month to ensure we are on track with our work?

The rationale for the other actions taking place this month, and in this order, include that an action is *more important* or needs doing *more urgently*, has a higher priority and therefore comes earlier in the month and vice versa. An action may be *part of a process* and so must happen before one action, but after another. Also, certain actions are *fixed* to events outside of the school's control and so these actions are tied to a particular date in the calendar (for example, external exams) or are actions *related to a fixed* event.

As the last month of schooling begins, it is worth noting that, if you hadn't noticed, time is now against you. There are as many actions to take in July as there were in June, but only 75% of the time. Being organised and efficient, without cutting corners, is key. So that everything that needs to be addressed in the summer holidays has been identified, the first thing to do is to check that the school continues to be compliant, and the school environment and website is as good as it can be. Anything that needs to be ordered for use at the start of the summer holidays can be ordered, minimising any delays.

Drawing together the various threads of the school year in July starts with a last update and evaluation of your faculty and school Improvement Plans. Chronologically next is preparing the celebration of exam results (July for Key Stage 2, August for Key Stage 4 and 5) and next year's start of term arrangements, distributing initial timetable, rooming, and routines and duties proposals. This is followed by the raft of work to be actioned in September, but so close to the beginning that considered preparation can only happen in July. This is true for updating the Schemes of Work and Programmes of Study, the Assessment and monitoring and tracking programmes, the School Policies, and the Assemblies and Inspiring Minds Programme. Early preparation for Open Evening and Open Week will take some of the pressure off in September, with a final reflection on the staff recruitment process and procedures and the integrated work of the school.

With so much in preparation, it is important not to lose sight of delivering a first-rate induction programme for staff and pupils new to the school; confirm and distribute the masterpieces that are the final school timetable, revised staff handbook, updated prospectus, job descriptions, and school calendar for any last-minute feedback.

Finally ... celebrate the end of term and the end of another school year!

 (All leaders)   **Evaluate all statutory requirements**

Securing progress by knowing that the education provided by you is compliant and up to date

As the academic year draws to a close, take a moment to consider the journey your school is making with regard to all statutory requirements being in place and the school's website being up to date. To help cross-reference how successful the school has been with the website and over the year in meeting the statutory requirements, the Department for Education (DfE) and The Key offer some useful insights and their website gives some useful guidance. More information on these can be found in Chapter 15 at the end of this book. In addition, using online tools such as Survey Monkey or Google Forms enables you to efficiently evaluate your work, saving you precious time. Use the following as an agenda or structure to help write your report and ensure that you have covered these key points.

Analyse

- What went well and what has not gone as well as hoped over the year with regard to all statutory requirements being in place?

- How does this compare to previous years?

- What positive messages/patterns and areas/patterns for improvement about learning, teaching, and leadership come out of this?

Evaluate

- What targets/goals were set to be achieved in relation to all statutory requirements being in place and have these targets/goals been achieved, partially achieved, or not achieved?

- What went well and what could have been improved? Have you consulted with key staff involved in the process and enabled them to give their views in relation to all statutory requirements being in place?

■ What are the reasons behind any successes and any areas that were less successful?

Action

■ What follow-up actions related to learning, teaching, and leadership need to be made, or key messages communicated as a result of your analysis/evaluation?

Celebrate

■ Arrange a method of celebrating success with regard to all statutory requirements being in place. Send letters of appreciation to key teachers and leaders for their notable positive contribution.

 (Senior leaders)   Evaluate the school environment

 Securing progress by having a high-quality working environment

As the academic year draws to a close, take a moment to review your working environment. Use the following as an agenda or structure to help write your report and ensure that you have covered these key points.

PREMISES	ALL WELL	NEEDING IMPROVEMENT (HOW)
Classrooms		
Decoration/flooring		
Displays		
Electrics and lighting		
Furniture and storage		
Heating		
Offices		
Preparation rooms		
Security		
Telephones, interactive whiteboards (IWBs) and personal computers (PCs)		
Toilets		
Windows		

(All leaders)   Update and evaluate Improvement Plans

Securing progress through improved learning, teaching and leadership

An important priority, before the end of the year, is to gather any final evidence and incorporate that into your faculty or school Improvement Plans, so that, ahead of the results in August, you have all the data you need at your fingertips.

To help cross-reference how successful the faculty, school Improvement Plans and continuing professional development (CPD) programme have been over the school year, Bubb and Earley (2009), Dunford (2016), and Ofsted (2019b) offer some useful insights and the DfE, Secondary Schools and Academies Trust (SSAT), and The Key on their websites give some useful guidance. More information on these can be found in Chapter 15 at the end of this book. In addition, using online tools such as Survey Monkey or Google Forms enables you to efficiently evaluate your work, saving you precious time. Use the following as an agenda or structure to help complete your plans and ensure that you have covered these key points.

Analyse

- What went well and what has not gone as well as hoped over the year with regard to your school/department's work?

- How does this compare to previous years?

- What positive messages/patterns and areas/patterns for improvement about learning, teaching, and leadership come out of this?

Evaluate

- What targets/goals were set to be achieved and have these targets/goals been achieved, partially achieved, or not achieved?

- What went well and what could have been improved? Have you consulted with key staff involved in the process and enabled them to give their views?

- What are the reasons behind any successes and any areas that were less successful?

Action

- What follow-up actions related to learning, teaching, and leadership need to be made, or key messages communicated as a result of your analysis/evaluation?

(Senior leaders) Finalise annual celebrations

Securing progress through celebrating and publicising pupil progress in their exams

Use the following and August's "Exam results" checklist ahead of any communications to help inform the celebration of the annual exams in July (Key Stage 2) and August (Key Stages 4 and 5).

▧ Have "Celebration of the annual exams" as an agenda item and get as many views as is reasonable to ensure you get a strong understanding of what needs to be done to have a fantastic, memorable celebration!

▧ Identify and agree any work to be done over the coming weeks.

▧ Save time: Use last year's information/guidance that went out and amend it to what you need.

▧ Propose the best: Provide a proposal that incorporates research and shares best practice in what you do, e.g. in staff In-Service Education and Training (INSET) / CPD.

▧ Propose the most workable solution: Pilot your proposal with a few trusted colleagues to give you feedback on your proposal. This will ensure that your proposal is as successful as it can be.

▧ Keep it flexible: Once your proposal is live, welcome feedback on what is going well and how it could be improved further. Review and tweak accordingly. Put out the final version when ready.

 (All leaders) Finalise start of year arrangements / routines

Securing progress by knowing the school community works efficiently and effectively

To help prepare the best end and starts of terms, explore what others have written or are doing. The DfE (2020b) offer some useful insights and the DfE, The Key, and others on their websites give some useful guidance. More information on these can be found in Chapter 15 at the end of this book. Also, use online tools such as Google Docs or Google Sheets to work on key documents or data concurrently with your team and ensure you work as effectively as possible. Use the following ahead of any communications to help inform the start of term arrangements and the school routines/process you expect to see in place in the new school year.

- Have "Review of start of school year/school routines" as an agenda item and get as many views as is reasonable to ensure you get a strong understanding of what needs to be done to have a smooth start to the year and effective routines in place next term.

- Identify and agree any work to be done over the summer holidays and at the start of the next term, including updates to the website.

- Save time: Use last year's information/guidance that went out and amend it to what you need.

- Propose the best: Provide a proposal that incorporates research and shares best practice in what you do, e.g. in staff INSET/CPD.

- Propose the most workable solution: Pilot your proposal with a few trusted colleagues to give you feedback on your proposal. This will ensure that your proposal is as successful as it can be.

- Keep it flexible: Once your proposal is live, welcome feedback on what is going well and how it could be improved further. Review and tweak accordingly. Put out the final version when ready.

> **(All leaders) Update Schemes of Work for Autumn 1**
> *Securing progress by providing a comprehensive, clear, and achievable curriculum*

To help prepare the best Schemes of Work and long-term plans, explore what others have written or are doing. Ofsted (2017) and Harpham (2020) offer some useful insights and The Key, exam boards, or the Times Educational Supplement (TES) on their websites give some useful guidance. More information on these can be found in Chapter 15 at the end of this book. Also, use online tools such as Google Docs or Google Sheets to work on key documents or data concurrently with your team and ensure you work as effectively as possible. As you review/ prepare your scheme of work for the autumn term, use the following to check it is as good as it can be:

- Are the **aims** of the scheme of work and each lesson **realistically high**, **clearly articulated**, and **ordered coherently** so progress over the scheme of work is **explicit**?

- Is the work to be completed **manageable**, **challenging**, and **consistently focused on pupil learning**?

- Is there explicit **progression in understanding** from description and facts to analysis and reasoning?

- Is there a clear **increase in the challenge/complexity of knowledge and skills** being learnt?

- Is the work expected to be completed **increasingly longer and harder**?

- Are activities progressing **from the class/group** to the **individual** over time and do they **include homework**?

- Is the **assessment for learning built into each lesson** and does it move **from informal to formal assessment**?

- What **provisions are in place** should anyone fall behind, or finish sooner than expected?

 (All leaders)   **Update the Assessment programme**

Securing progress by having a way of assessing learning that is best practice and effective

---

To help prepare the best Assessment programme, explore what others have written or are doing. Christodoulou (2016) and Wiliam (2018) offer some useful insights and the DfE (2016c), the Education Endowment Foundation (EEF) and PiXL on their websites give some useful guidance. More information on these can be found in Chapter 15 at the end of this book. Also, use online tools such as Google Docs or Google Sheets to work on key documents or data concurrently with your team and ensure you work as effectively as possible.

- Have "Update to the Assessment programme" as an agenda item and get as many views as is reasonable to ensure you get a strong understanding of what needs to be done to have a smooth start to the year and effective routines in place next term.

- Identify and agree any work to be done over the summer holidays and at the start of the next term.

- Save time: Use last year's information/guidance that went out and amend it to what you need.

- Propose the best: provide a proposal that incorporates research and shares best practice in what you do, e.g. in staff INSET/CPD.

- Propose the most workable solution: Pilot your proposal with a few trusted colleagues to give you feedback on your proposal. This will ensure that your proposal is as successful as it can be.

▓ Keep it flexible: Once your proposal is live, welcome feedback on what is going well and how it could be improved further. Review and tweak accordingly. Put out the final version when ready.

Use the following ahead of any communications to help inform the updating of the Assessment programme, so that it is as good as it can be and in place in time for the new school year.

Grade predictions

To ensure your grade predictions are as reliable as they can be, consider the following.

Reliable grade prediction = rigorous data collection + rigorous quality assurance

Rigorous data collection incorporates each of the following:

Standardised test grades (Objective/independent)

Useful to include as they are standardised with other schools and are set independent of the teacher.

Homework grades (Subjective/ independent)

Useful to include as they indicate how well the pupil can work independently.

Teacher assessment (Subjective /dependent)

Useful to include as they indicate how well the pupil responds to guidance

Rigorous quality assurance ensures:

Programmes of Study and Schemes of Work are up to date and comprehensive.

Programmes of Study and Schemes of Work have been checked against the exam specification.

The pace of teaching and learning in the Schemes of Work and Programmes of Study is sufficient.

To ensure your grade predictions are as reliable as they can be, ensure you have rigorous data collection and quality assurance procedures in place throughout the year.

Moments that count in July: An unexpected encounter

Senior Citizens Tea Party in Wray Crescent Park, Islington. A more sedate version of a summer music festival in a park; average age in attendance, 70 years and counting. What is similar though is that it is an annual event that is enjoyed by those attending and those facilitating. My students are given the opportunity to practice our cornerstone of respect through serving others and being kind to the old folks for an afternoon; their thoughts, not mine.

As Headteacher, you have to be the spokesperson for your school and say something at any event, sometimes at the drop of a hat. I was focused on downing a cheese and tomato sandwich that I was dying to eat as my stomach had sunk to new lows due to the hunger pains, which up until this point, I was far too busy to address.

I was called upon to do just that. I spoke glowingly with pride and congratulated my young people on their ability to make great sandwiches and entertain our guests. Afterwards, I milled around meeting and greeting, but looking at my watch, knowing that I had to be somewhere else, doing something else of great importance, sometime soon. Where is your PA when you need her?! I left and went back to school (the park is opposite the school) filled with warm thoughts of the mutual gratitude that I just witnessed, providing the opportunity to grow responsible adults with an understanding of the worth of others who are unlike them. To care.

The next day, the receptionist came into my office and brought in a napkin which had been handed in to reception for me. It came from one of the carers that had accompanied a senior citizen from their care home. This lady, a former tutee in my early years of leadership had spoken to me at the function before I left. It read:

"Dear Ms Service (Forgive this napkin)

I didn't expect to ever see you again, that has made me smile. I wanted you to know as a teacher and mentor I've never forgotten you. I really feel like you were one teacher who cared about their students (and I was right because now you're head!!) I am so happy for you and feel so proud you were my teacher. I am now studying to be a nurse and somehow that is still down to you and your impression you left on me. I hope this doesn't offend you but growing up with the family I did (White Irish) you was the first strong, funny and smart black woman I met and again for that I will always remember you.

Many thanks for my schooling years, You're amazing.

All the best"

We must never forget that this profession counts at all times because it makes a difference to people's lives, and I know that I made a difference to at least one person's life.

Susan Service, Headteacher

(All leaders)   Review monitoring and tracking

Securing success by routinely checking that everyone is making expected progress

To help prepare the best monitoring and tracking programme, explore what others have written or are doing. Nasen (2014), McClusky (2017), and the EEF (2018) offer some useful insights and the EEF and the Fisher Family Trust on their websites give some useful guidance. More information on these can be found in Chapter 15 at the end of this book. Also, use online tools such as Google Docs or Google Sheets to work on key documents or data concurrently with your team and ensure you work as effectively as possible. Use the following ahead of any communications to help ensure the monitoring and tracking programme is as up to date and effective as it can be in the new school year.

- Have "Review of monitoring and tracking programme" as an agenda item and get as many views as is reasonable to ensure you get a strong understanding of what needs to be done to have a smooth start to the year and effective routines in place next term.

- Identify and agree any work to be done over the summer holidays and at the start of the next term.

- Save time: Use last year's information/guidance that went out and amend it to what you need.

- Propose the best: Provide a proposal that incorporates research and shares best practice in what you do, e.g. in staff INSET/CPD.

- Propose the most workable solution: Pilot your proposal with a few trusted colleagues to give you feedback on your proposal. This will ensure that your proposal is as successful as it can be.

- Keep it flexible: Once your proposal is live, welcome feedback on what is going well and how it could be improved further. Review and tweak accordingly. Put out the final version when ready.

 (Senior leaders) Update all key policies

Securing progress through providing a compliant educational experience for all

To help prepare the best policies, explore what others have written or are doing. Law (2000) and the DfE (2014c) offer some useful insights and Hub4Leaders and Policies for Schools on their websites give some useful guidance. More information on these can be found in Chapter 15 at the end of this book. Also, use online tools such as Google Docs or Google Sheets to work on key documents or data concurrently with your team and ensure you work as effectively as possible. Use the following ahead of any communications to help ensure that all policies that need updating ahead of the start of term are being updated in time for the new school year.

■ Have "School policies update" as an agenda item and get as many views as is reasonable to ensure you get a strong understanding of what needs to be done to have a smooth start to the year and effective routines in place next term.

■ Identify and agree any work to be done over the summer holidays and at the start of the next term.

■ Save time: Use last year's information/guidance that went out and amend it to what you need.

■ Propose the best: Provide a proposal that incorporates research and shares best practice in what you do, e.g. in staff INSET/CPD.

■ Propose the most workable solution: Pilot your proposal with a few trusted colleagues to give you feedback on your proposal. This will ensure that your proposal is as successful as it can be.

■ Keep it flexible: Once your proposal is live, welcome feedback on what is going well and how it could be improved further. Review and tweak accordingly. Put out the final version when ready.

An electronic copy of this Policies checklist can be found and downloaded from the School Leader's Resources page at: www.schoolleaderdevelopment.com.

POLICY	STATUTORY	FREQUENCY OF REVIEW
16–19 Bursary	N	1 yearly
Abusive Parents	N	2 yearly
Accessibility and Disability	Y	3 yearly
Admissions	Y	1 yearly
Alcohol, Drugs, and Gambling at Work	N	3 yearly
Anti-Bullying	N	3 yearly
Assessment, Marking, and Feedback	N	2 yearly
Attendance	Y	1 yearly
Behaviour	Y	2 yearly
Capability Procedure	Y	2 yearly
CCTV	N	3 yearly
Centre Assessments of External Qualifications	Y	1 yearly

POLICY	STATUTORY	FREQUENCY OF REVIEW
Charging and Remissions	Y	2 yearly
Child Protection	Y	1 yearly
Children Looked After	N	1 yearly
Code of Conduct	Y	3 yearly
Collective Worship	N	3 yearly
Complaints	Y	2 yearly
Contract of Employment for School Support Staff	N	1 yearly
Controlled Assessments	N	3 yearly
Cover	N	1 yearly
Data Protection	Y	3 yearly
Disciplinary	Y	3 yearly
Drugs and Substance Abuse	N	3 yearly
Emergency Evacuation Procedures	N	3 yearly
Equality (including Disability and Race)	Y	3 yearly
Exams 14–19	N	4 yearly
Flexible Working	N	2 yearly
Freedom of Information	Y	2 yearly
Grievance	Y	3 yearly
Guidance for the Management of Work-Related Stress	N	2 yearly
Harassment and Bullying	Y	3 yearly
Health and Attendance	N	3 yearly
Health and Safety	Y	3 yearly
Homework	N	3 yearly
International Policy	N	2 yearly
Leave of Absence	N	3 yearly
Lettings	N	1 yearly
Literacy	N	2 yearly
Manual of Financial Procedures and Regulations	N	1 yearly
Maternity, Paternity, Adoption, and Carer's Guide	N	2 yearly
Numeracy	N	2 yearly
Off-site Visits	N	2 yearly
Pay and Performance Appraisal – Teachers and Support Staff	Y	2 yearly
Probationary Period for Support Staff	N	3 yearly
Race Equality Policy	N	3 yearly
Restrictive Physical Intervention	N	3 yearly
Safeguarding Checklist	N	1 yearly
Safer Recruitment	N	Ongoing
Safety and Data Security	N	3 yearly
Schedule of Financial Delegation	N	1 yearly
Searching, Screening, and Confiscation	N	2 yearly
Security	Y	2 yearly
SEND	Y	2 yearly
Sex Education and Relationships	Y	2 yearly
Shared Parental Leave	N	2 yearly
Shared Parental Leave Toolkit	N	2 yearly
Stress Management and Employee Wellbeing	N	3 yearly
Supporting Pupils with Medical Conditions	N	1 yearly
Teaching and Learning	N	1 yearly
Uniform	N	3 yearly
Whistleblowing	N	3 yearly

Updating four key areas

To help prepare these next four key activities for next term, take some time to refer to what others have written or published on websites that either confirm that what you are doing is best practice, or offer guidance as to how the school's practice might be improved. Each of the activities and some related documents and websites are presented in the table below.

More information on these can be found in Chapter 15 at the end of this book. In addition, using online tools such as Survey Monkey or Google Forms enables you to efficiently evaluate your work, saving you precious time. For each of the activities in the table below, use the bullet points after the table to ensure that you have covered these key points in any reports or communications.

LEADERS	UPDATE ACTIVITY	KEY DOCUMENTS	WEBSITES
All	The new assembly rota & new Inspiring Minds programme	Foster (2017) and Sedgwick (2006)	DfE, TES, BBC Assemblies.org.uk
All	Open Evening and Open Week programme	N/A	The Key, The Good Schools Guide, LEAs
All	Staff recruitment process and procedures	DfE (2019a)	DfE, The Key, Teach First
All	The budget and the integrated work of the school	Percival (2006), DfE (2020a)	The Key and the DfE

- Have these update activities as an agenda item and get as many views as is reasonable to ensure you get a strong understanding of what needs to be done to deliver best practice, e.g. in staff INSET/CPD.

- Identify and agree any work to be done over the summer holidays and at the start of the next term.

- Save time: Use last year's information/guidance that went out and amend it to what you need.

- Propose the best: Provide a proposal that incorporates research and shares best practice in what you do, e.g. in staff INSET/CPD.

- Propose the most workable solution: Pilot your proposal with a few trusted colleagues to give you feedback on your proposal. This will ensure that your proposal is as successful as it can be.

■ Keep it flexible: Once your proposal is live, welcome feedback on what is going well and how it could be improved further. Review and tweak accordingly. Put out the final version when ready.

 (All leaders)   Deliver induction and finalise Summer School

Securing progress by getting everyone into good working/learning habits right from the start

Before you get your induction team to work, or you make your presentation to others, use the following to help check that you have covered all the actions that are needed for staff and pupil induction to be a success:

■ Have you clearly articulated what you and others need to do, and when and where regarding induction?

■ What is the deadline for the work to be completed?

■ What clear milestones are to be reached along the way?

■ If this is additional to people's work, what should they do about covering their other work that is being missed?

■ What should people do if there is a problem?

 (Senior leaders)   Distribute key documents to staff

Securing progress by knowing the school community works efficiently and effectively

The end of the term and the school year is almost here.

Distribute the final (well, almost final) versions of the timetable, School Calendar, and duty rota and a copy of the finalised handbook, prospectus, job descriptions, new staff list, and meetings schedule for final comments.

■ Have you clearly articulated what you and others need to do, and when and where regarding the key documents?

■ What is the deadline for any feedback/questions to be sent?

■ What should people do if there is a problem?

(All leaders) **Action celebrations and end of term arrangements**

Securing progress through recognising and celebrating the progress made over the year

Just before you crack open a bottle of something to celebrate the end of the school year, there is one final job that needs to be done: Sign off the progress of the new teachers on their support programme for this term. Key questions that will help evaluate this include the following:

Attendance and punctuality: Has their attendance/punctuality rate been high or dropped below expectations?

Professionalism: Have they behaved in line with the school's Code of Conduct, or have there been issues?

Teachers' standards: Is there sufficient evidence to say they are on track to successfully meet the standards?

Evidence: Has someone checked that all the evidence that should be in place is in place?

Concerns: Are there any concerns that need addressing in the summer term?

Once all is in order, these need to be signed off and sent to the local authority/relevant university/training body and a celebration had of the progress the trainee/new teachers have made this term.

The end of the school year is here and deserves to be recognised and acknowledged. Applaud the work of the whole school community! Here are some points to bear in mind as you celebrate the end of the year:

- Arrange a suitable and appropriate method of celebrating success for the whole school (See Prize Giving in June) and year groups in end of year assemblies.

- Publish social media posts, a press release, an article for the school's newsletter/website with your good news.

- Write letters of appreciation to key teachers and leaders for their notable positive contribution.

- Make explicit the progress you are making as a school.

Moments that count in July: End of term

July. It has always been a momentous month on the school calendar. The Reception or Year 7 cohort finishing up their first year as the babies of the school; Year 6 or Year 11 pupils gone, having finished their exams with their sights set on a bright future; dedicated staff yearning for a well-deserved break, some counting down to retirement, or pastures new.

But for a behaviour specialist like me, the month of July has always been a good opportunity to look back and reflect on the myriad of pastoral issues schools face – particularly with some of the most challenging and vulnerable children in our care. For many of them: on a tightrope: of successful learning outcomes, or permanent exclusion.

One particular child, who we'll call Ollie, joined us via a managed move. This was his last chance. His previous school had written him off due to countless exclusions and the breakdowns in relationships he had accrued.

"Give it 'til half-term", Ollie's previous Headteacher said to me. But I was not so sure …

Ollie had a spark and strong academic potential; it was just unfortunate that a traumatic upbringing and poor choices had derailed him. I was certain that by believing in him and providing the right support, there were better days ahead.

Thursday 20th July – 9 months or so down the line, I pondered in my office – what had become of Ollie since starting with us? This once troubled pain-in-the-neck worked hard for a successful transition into our school which had the right set of principles to nurture a child like him; having made key friend-ships with his peers in the year group, he built strong relationships with his class teachers and was working to "above expected" progress in the majority of his subject areas.

There was no doubt that as a school we were not there yet with Ollie. He was a child that would need targeted-interventions for the foreseeable future in order for him to embrace becoming a self-regulating learner and effectively communicate the many issues he had been through, or the pressures he would face growing up in an inner-London area with problems of its own.

Whilst for any school, there will always be an overarching objective of securing good results and good data, for pastoral leaders it is these moments that count, where lives can be transformed through a strong pastoral system, inclusion and an embedded ethos that every child, whether at school or at home, can be a champion.

David Ritchie, Assistant Head

Summary and checklist for July

LEADER ACTION	FOCUS	SENIOR LEADERS	MIDDLE LEADERS
Analyse and Applaud	All statutory requirements		
	The school environment/display areas		
	Final update of Improvement Plans (FIP/SIP/SEF/CPD)		▓
Arrange	Prepare celebration of exam results		
	Prepare next year's start of term/routines/duties	▓	
	Update Schemes of Work for Autumn Term I (AUTI) and Programmes of Study		
	Update Assessment programme		
	Update monitoring and tracking programme		
	Update School Policies		▓
	Update Assemblies and Inspiring Minds Programme		▓
	Review and arrange Open Evening and Open Week		
	Update staff recruitment process and procedures		▓
	Update integrated work of the school		▓
Action	Deliver pupil and staff induction and begin Summer School		
	Distribute Timetable/Handbook/Prospectus/Job Descriptions/Calendar		▓
	Implement end of term arrangements		

August

You've made it!

The year has drawn to a close.

August is a month of drawing breath, celebrating the wonderful achievements of a lifetime for some treasured pupils.

DOI: 10.4324/9781003129691-15

Introduction: August

With the school's day-to-day educational work coming to a close, August is the month to gather and draw breath. For most school leaders, it allows some much-needed time off for a few weeks before addressing the annual results. Once these are in, essentially school leaders, especially senior leaders, are back to work. Here is what you have in store for August.

AUGUST SUMMARY							
KEY							
	Action that analyses, evaluates, and celebrates previous work		》》	Action that supports current work		↻	Action that prepares future work
Statutory activity (higher priority)				Non-statutory activity (lower priority)			
Action	Leaders	School focus for August					
》》	Senior leaders	Deliver Summer School programme					
》》	Senior leaders	Complete maintenance programme and confirm compliance					
》》	All leaders	Celebrate annual exam results					

The rationale for the other actions taking place this month, and in this order, include that an action is *more important* or needs doing *more urgently*, has a higher priority and therefore comes earlier in the month and vice versa. An action may be *part of a process* and so must happen before one action, but after another. Also, certain actions are *fixed* to events outside of the school's control and so these actions are tied to a particular date in the calendar (for example, external exams), or are actions *related to a fixed* event.

As the corridors and classrooms fall silent of the usual stampede of pupils moving to lessons, new sounds can be heard, with the arrival of new pupils settling in through their Summer School experience, the steady hum of repairs and maintenance across the site, and the sobs and cheers as the annual results come in and are distributed. And so, closes another school year.

》》 **(Senior leaders)   Deliver Summer School programme**

Securing progress by getting everyone into good working/learning habits right from the start

---

Before you get your Summer School team to work, or you make your presentation to others, use the following to help check that you have covered all the actions that are needed for the Summer School to be a success:

- Have you clearly articulated what you and others need to do, and when and where regarding Summer School?

- If this is additional to people's work, what should they do about covering their other work that is being missed?

- What should people do if there is a problem?

》》》 (Senior leaders) Complete repairs and confirm compliance

An improved working environment increases the chances of pupils achieving success

---

Ensuring efficient and effective use of the summer break to get all the required work done as quickly as possible is in everyone's best interest. Having a clear plan of action/Gant chart right from the start will ensure no false starts and everyone can get on with the job from the first. Before you get your repairs and maintenance team working, use the following to help check that you have covered all the actions that are needed to be a success:

- Have you clearly articulated what you and others need to do, and when and where?

- Have you prioritised the statutory work, for example, health and safety (doors, steps, lighting, heating, water, or toilets), security (entry systems and fencing), and complex work such as technology and telephones?

- What is the deadline for each piece of work to be completed?

- What clear milestones are to be reached along the way?

- If this is additional to people's work, what should they do about covering their other work that is being missed?

- What should people do if there is a problem?

》》》 (All leaders) Celebrate the annual exam results with pupils

Securing progress through celebrating and publicising pupil progress in their exams

---

Before the exam results are in and you get your exam team mobilised, use the following to help check that you have covered all the actions that are needed to be a success:

- Have you clearly articulated what you and others need to do, and when and where?

- Have they got all the resources and skills they need to do the work?

- If not, what resources or training will be provided to enable them to do the job?

- What is the timeframe for the work to be completed?

- What clear milestones are to be reached along the way?

- If this is additional to people's work, what should they do about covering their other work that is being missed?

- What should people do if there is a problem?

On the day, use the following to check all is in place:

- Have a box of tissues handy.

- Have the Careers adviser and information about local employers/universities present and handy.

- Book in a photographer.

- Contact local newspapers.

- Book in key people for the day before to analyse the results.

- Lay on cakes and coffee to keep the wheels turning smoothly.

- Have a plan of action for the what ifs: What if I do not get one of the grades I need; what if I don't get two of the grades I need; what if I don't get any of the grades I need?

- Have a clear line of response to parents and pupils who do not get the grades and want answers from the school.

- Identify the best pupils, check that they are coming in, and prepare them to give a quote.

- Set a time to arrange a photo opportunity.

- Draft a press release the night before – include top achievers and top pupils who have made great progress.

Five ways forward if pupils do not make the grade

- **Appeal**: If they achieve 1–2% below the grade above, a re-mark should be considered.
- **Call**: Contact each university to see if a place is still possible on the course of choice.
- **Change**: Contact each university to see if a place is still possible on similar courses.
- **Take a chance**: Go through clearing and see if other universities have availability.
- **Try again**: Consider a year out/additional time to re-take and try again next year.

- Celebrate with every pupil – it is their big day and will not ever happen again – make it special!

- Make sure to get the best/most interesting pupils for the photograph line up.

- Celebrate your news on your website and social media.

- Carefully craft your message like a finely tailored dress or suit – it accentuates the positive without actually being fake!

Summary and checklist for August

LEADER ACTION	FOCUS	SENIOR LEADERS	MIDDLE LEADERS
Action	Deliver Summer School programme		
	Complete the repairs/maintenance programme and confirm compliance		
	Celebrate annual exam results		

Concluding thoughts

So here we are at the end of the school year and the end of this book.

Since starting to write this book, the UK has left the EU, a pandemic has swept across the world, and school buildings and playgrounds have been empty for over a year. The shock waves created and currently being managed by teachers and school leaders in their school communities have been profound but will eventually diminish in time.

However, two things that appear set to continue as major influences on education are government directives and the advances made by education in using information technology to deliver more hybrid or blended remote teaching and learning.

With government demands and their agenda continuing to frequently change, there appears to be no end in sight, nor let-up in the pressure under which school leaders have to work. Similarly, with little significant change in the way school success is judged, the continuing emphasis on performativity and the need for schools to deliver results under, and by, whatever circumstances continues unabated.

However, following COVID-19 and the imperative for education to join the global information technological revolution, school leaders have the largest repertoire of strategies to deliver high-quality, effective teaching and learning than ever before. The genie is truly out of the bottle and education has truly moved online; no longer is it assessment for, or of learning, but the experience can be viewed as assessment for, or of online learning. The future for the school leader then is not just school leadership, but leadership of online schooling. Sir Tim Berners-Lee and his creation, the internet, has truly come of age.

If you are a school leader new to post, I hope the thoughts presented in this book gave you some guidance as to how to lead more effectively and increase the potential for progress being made with the leaders, teachers, and pupils under your care.

If you are an experienced school leader, I hope this book has provided some external validation for the decisions and choices you make, in effectively leading your department or school.

As a result of reading this book, I hope these ideas have helped in some way to make your interactions with those with whom you work, their progress, and your leadership more effective and more successful.

In the spirit of this book, I would love to hear your feedback. You can contact me at michael@schoolleaderdevelopment.com.

I look forward to hearing from you.

Suggested websites

Below are suggested websites that provide further useful information and reference with regard to each of the key areas needing to be led.

ACTIVITY	ORGANISATION	WEBSITE ADDRESS
Admissions	Department for Education	www.gov.uk/schools-admissions
	Local Education Authority	See individual Local Education Authority (LEA) e.g. Hertfordshire
	Eadmissions	www.eadmissions.org.uk
	Good Schools Guide	www.goodschoolsguide.co.uk
Appeals (exams)	Department for Education	www.gov.uk/appeal-qualification-result
	JCQ	www.jcq.org.uk/exams-office/appeals
	Exam boards, e.g. AQA	See exam board website (see Exams)
Assemblies	Department for Education	www.gov.uk/government/publications/collective-worship-in-schools
	Assemblies.org.uk	www.assemblies.org.uk
	Assembly Box	https://assemblybox.co.uk
	TES	www.tes.com/teaching-resources/blog/assembly-ideas-academic-year
	BBC: R/KS1/2 Assemblies	www.bbc.co.uk/programmes/p00nkdgx
Assessment	Department for Education (Assessment principles)	www.gov.uk/government/publications/assessment-principles-school-curriculum
	Department for Education (National Curriculum)	www.gov.uk/government/publications/national-curriculum-and-assessment-information-for-schools
	PiXL	www.pixl.org.uk/about-us
	EEF	https://educationendowmentfoundation.org.uk/tools/assessing-and-monitoring-pupil-progress/developing-whole-school-assessment

ACTIVITY	ORGANISATION	WEBSITE ADDRESS
Budget	Department for Education (Financial Handbook)	www.gov.uk/guidance/academies-finan cial-handbook/academies-financial-h andbook-2020-to-print
	Department for Education (Pupil Premium Funding)	DfE Pupil Premium funding and accountability for schools
	The Key	https://schoolleaders.thekeysupport .com/administration-and-management/ financial-management/budget/
	School Business support services	www.schoolbusinessservices.co.uk/fi nance-support
Capital bids	Department for Education	www.gov.uk/guidance/school-capital- funding
	Grantsonline	www.grantsonline.org.uk
	Grants4schools	www.grants4schools.info
Careers	Department for Education	www.gov.uk/government/publications/ careers-guidance-provision-for-young -people-in-schools
	UCAS	www.ucas.com/further-education/post -16-finance-and-support/careers-inf ormation-and-guidance-schools
	Careers Inc	www.careersinc.uk/basecopy/virtual- careers-advice
Catch Up and revision programmes	BBC Bitesize	www.bbc.co.uk/bitesize
	EEF	https://educationendowmentfoundation .org.uk
	Get Revising	https://getrevising.co.uk
	Khan Academy	www.khanacademy.org/
	PIXL	www.pixl.org.uk/about-us
	SAM Learning	www.samlearning.com
	TES Teaching resources	www.tes.com/teaching-resources
	Word wall	https://wordwall.net
Census	Department for Education	https://www.gov.uk/government/publi cations/school-census-2020-to-2021- technical-information
	Local Education Authority	See individual LEA e.g. Hertfordshire
End/start of term	Department for Education (COVID safe start to term)	https://assets.publishing.service.gov.uk /government/uploads/system/uploads/ attachment_data/file/899384/Checkli st_for_school_leaders_on_behaviour_ and_attendance.pdf
	M. Busy teacher.org	https://m.busyteacher.org/11603-last-les son-10-ideas-end-year.html
	The Key	https://schoolleaders.thekeysupport .com/administration-and-management/ structuring-school-day-year/restructurin g-the-school-year-maintained-schools

(Continued)

ACTIVITY	ORGANISATION	WEBSITE ADDRESS
Exams and coursework (KS1 and 2)	IXL	https://uk.ixl.com/promo?partner =google&campaign=1187&adGroup =Key+Stage+2&gclid=CPPa8teS _8kCFQbnwgodgOIB6A
	BBC	www.bbc.co.uk/education
	Education Quizzes	www.educationquizzes.com/ks2/maths/
	Mad for Maths	www.mad4maths.com/
	Key Stage 2 Literacy	www.keystage2literacy.co.uk/spellings -menu.html
Exams and coursework (KS4 and 5)	JCQ	www.jcq.org.uk
	AQA	www.aqa.org.uk
	Edexcel	https://qualifications.pearson.com/en/ho me.html
	OCR	www.ocr.org.uk
	WJEC	www.wjec.co.uk
Improvement Plans and SEF	SSAT	www.ssatuk.co.uk/cpd/school -improvement/
	The Key	https://thekeysupport.com/the-key
	Blue Sky	www.blueskyeducation.co.uk
Induction	The Key Pupil induction (Primary)	https://schoolleaders.thekeysupport .com/pupils-and-parents/pupil-health -and-wellbeing/pupil-transitions-and-pa storal-systems/induction-packs-for-new -pupils-primary
	The Key Pupil induction (Secondary)	https://schoolleaders.thekeysupport .com/covid-19/safeguard-and-support -pupils/pupil-wellbeing-and-mental-healt h/coronavirus-supporting-pupil-transitio n-to-secondary
	Department for Education (Induction for NQTs)	https://assets.publishing.service.gov.uk /government/uploads/system/uploads/ attachment_data/file/923070/Statutory _Induction_Guidance_2019.pdf
	The Key Staff induction	https://schoolleaders.thekeysupport .com/staff/recruitment-and-induction/ind uction/staff-induction-guide-checklist
Integrated Framework	Department for Education	www.gov.uk/government/collections/s chools-financial-health-and-efficiency
Leavers	Teachwire (Primary)	www.teachwire.net/news/5-of-the-best -activities-and-resources-for-primary-s chool-leavers
	Twinkl (Primary)	www.twinkl.co.uk/resource/t2-e-41368 -year-6-leavers-project-activity-pack
	Department for Education	www.gov.uk/know-when-you-can-leave- school

(Continued)

ACTIVITY	ORGANISATION	WEBSITE ADDRESS
Monitoring and Tracking	EEF	https://educationendowmentfoundation.org.uk
	Fisher Family Trust	https://fft.org.uk/pupil-tracking
	Pupil Progress	www.pupilprogress.com
Open Evening and displays	The Key	https://schoolleaders.thekeysupport.com/covid-19/manage-regular-school-business/coronavirus-how-safely-run-your-open-events
	The Good Schools Guide	www.goodschoolsguide.co.uk/choosing-a-school/school-open-days
	Local Education Authority	See individual LEA e.g. Hertfordshire
Options	Department for Education (National Curriculum)	www.gov.uk/government/collections/national-curriculum
	Department for Education (EBACC)	https://assets.publishing.service.gov.uk/government/uploads/system/uploads/attachment_data/file/761031/DfE_EBacc_Leaflet.pdf
	Ofqual	www.gov.uk/government/organisations/ofqual
Parents' Evenings	Groupcall	www.groupcall.com/product/messenger/messenger-parents-evenings
	ParentMail	www.parentmail.co.uk/services/parents-evening-manager
	SIMS	www.capita-sims.co.uk/products-and-services/parents-evening-system
Performance Appraisal	Department for Education	www.gov.uk/government/publications/teacher-appraisal-and-capability-model-policy
	The Key	https://schoolleaders.thekeysupport.com/staff/performance-management
	Blue Sky	www.blueskyeducation.co.uk
Policies	Department for Education	https://assets.publishing.service.gov.uk/government/uploads/system/uploads/attachment_data/file/357068/statutory_schools_policies_Sept_14_FINAL.pdf
	Department for Education	www.gov.uk/guidance/what-maintained-schools-must-publish-online
	Hub4leaders	https://hub4leaders.co.uk/learning-hub/model-policies-for-schools
	Policies for Schools	www.policiesforschools.co.uk/list-of-school-policies

(Continued)

ACTIVITY	ORGANISATION	WEBSITE ADDRESS
Pupil recruitment/ destinations	Department for Education	www.gov.uk/government/collections/s tatistics-destinations
	SIMS	www.capita-sims.co.uk/why-sims/attr acting-new-pupils
	Education Advisers	www.educationadvisers.co.uk/schools -services-pupil-recruitment
Quality assurance	Ofsted	https://assets.publishing.service.gov.uk /government/uploads/system/uploads/ attachment_data/file/843108/School_ inspection_handbook_-_section_5.pdf
	The Key	https://schoolleaders.thekeysupport .com/school-evaluation-and-improvem ent/inspection
	Local Education Authority	See individual LEA e.g. Hertfordshire
Repairs and maintenance	Department for Education	www.gov.uk/guidance/good-estate-man agement-for-schools/maintaining-the -estate
	Department for Education	*Essential School Maintenance: A guide for schools*
	Local Education Authority	See individual LEA e.g. Hertfordshire
Routines and duties	Department for Education	www.gov.uk/government/publications/ health-and-safety-advice-for-schools/res ponsibilities-and-duties-for-schools
	Health and Safety Executive	www.hse.gov.uk/services/education/i ndex.htm
	NSPCC	www.nspcc.org.uk/keeping-children-safe /away-from-home/at-school
Schemes of Work/ Programmes of Study	Department for Education	www.gov.uk/government/collections/ national-curriculum#programmes-of -study-by-subject
	The Key (R/KS1 and 2)	https://schoolleaders.thekeysupport .com/curriculum-and-learning/curric ulum-guidance-all-phases/structuring -curriculum/schemes-of-work-2014-c urriculum
	Scheme Support (Primary)	https://www.schemesupport.co.uk
	TES (Key Stages 3, 4, and 5)	https://www.tes.com/teaching-resources /blog/top-secondary-science-schemes -work
	Twinkl (Primary)	www.twinkl.co.uk/resource/t2-e-41368 -year-6-leavers-project-activity-pack
	Exam Boards	See **Exams** for KS4 and 5 Schemes of work laid out by your exam board

(Continued)

ACTIVITY	ORGANISATION	WEBSITE ADDRESS
Staff Handbook/ Prospectus	The Key	https://schoolleaders.thekeysupport .com/staff/recruitment-and-induction/ind uction/school-staff-handbook
	Simply Docs	https://simply-docs.co.uk/Employment -Polices-and-HR-Forms/Employment-a nd-Staff-Handbook-Policies?gclid=EA IaIQobChMIq5OFkqKC7gIVB57tCh38 8gmfEAMYAyAAEgIEMPD_BwE
Staff recruitment	Department for Education	www.gov.uk/government/publications/ teacher-recruitment-and-retention-s trategy
	The Key	https://schoolleaders.thekeysupport .com/staff/pay-and-progression/perf ormance-related-pay/recruitment-and -retention-payments-for-teachers
	Teach First	www.teachfirst.org.uk/schools
Statutory requirements	Department for Education	www.gov.uk/government/collections/s tatutory-guidance-schools
	Department for Education	https://assets.publishing.service.gov.uk /government/uploads/system/uploads/ attachment_data/file/357068/statutory _schools_policies_Sept_14_FINAL.pdf
	The Key	https://schoolleaders.thekeysupport .com/policy-bank/writing-school-policies /statutory-policies-documents-schools/
Summer Schools	Department for Education	www.gov.uk/government/publications/ the-impact-of-the-summer-schools-pr ogramme-on-pupils
	EEF	https://educationendowmentfoundation .org.uk/evidence-summaries/teaching-lea rning-toolkit/summer-schools
	NFER	www.nfer.ac.uk/publications/ESSP02/ ESSP02.pdf
Surveys	Ofsted Parent Questionnaire	https://parentview.ofsted.gov.uk/
	Ofsted Staff Questionnaire	https://assets.publishing.service.gov.uk /government/uploads/system/uploads/ attachment_data/file/674460/Staff_s urvey_questions_-_schools_-_January _2018.pdf
	Ofsted Pupil Questionnaire	https://assets.publishing.service.gov.uk /government/uploads/system/uploads/ attachment_data/file/674461/Pupil_s urvey_questions_-_schools_-_January _2018.pdf

(Continued)

ACTIVITY	ORGANISATION	WEBSITE ADDRESS
Tests	Department for Education (Stds and Testing Agency)	www.gov.uk/government/organisations/ standards-and-testing-agency
	Educake	www.educake.co.uk
	Kahoot	https://kahoot.com
	PIXL	www.pixl.org.uk/about-us
	Quizlet	https://quizlet.com/en-gb
	Socrative	www.socrative.com
Timetabling	MIST	www.mistservices.co.uk/services/tim etabling_course.aspx?servId=107
	SIMS	www.capita-sims.co.uk/products-and-services/sims-curriculum-management -suite
	Timetabler	www.timetabler.com

Bibliography

Anderson, L.W. and Krathwohl, D.R. (2001). *A Taxonomy for Learning, Teaching, and Assessing: A Revision of Bloom's Taxonomy of Educational Objectives*. London: Pearson.

Bambrick-Santoyo, P. (2018). *Leverage Leadership, 2.0: A Practical Guide to Building Exceptional Schools*. San Francisco, CA: Jossey-Bass.

Bennett, R.E. (2011). Formative assessment: A critical review, in *Assessment in Education: Principles, Policy and Practice*, 18(1), 5–25.

Biesta, G. (2008). Good education in an age of measurement: On the need to reconnect with the question of purpose in education, in *Educational Assessment, Evaluation and Accountability*, 21(1), 33–46.

Birbalsingh, K. (2016). *Battle Hymn of the Tiger Teachers: The Michaela Way*. Woodbridge: John Catt.

Blandford, S. (2000). *Managing Professional Development in Schools*. London: Routledge.

Bubb, S. and Earley, P. (2009). Leading staff development for school improvement, in *School Leadership and Management*, 29(1), 23–37.

Christodoulou, D. (2016). *Making Good Progress: The Future of Assessment for Learning*. Oxford: Oxford University Press.

Coates, S. (2015). *Head Strong: 11 Lessons in School Leadership*. Woodbridge: John Catt.

Coe, R., Aloisi, C., Higgins, S., and Elliot Major, L. (2014). *What Makes Great Teaching? Review of the Underpinning Research*. Sutton Trust.

Cooper Gibson Research (2017). *Understanding Schools' Responses to the Progress 8 Accountability Measure*. London: Department for Education.

Cordingley, P., Higgins, S., Greany, T., Buckler, N., Coles-Jordan, D., Crisp, B., Saunders, L., and Coe, R. (2015). *Developing Great Teaching: Lessons from the International Reviews into Effective Professional Development*. London: Teacher Development Trust.

Department for Education (1994). *Circular 1 / 94 – Religious Education and Collective Worship*. London: DfE.

Department for Education (2011). *Teachers' Standards*. London: DfE.

Department for Education (2013). *Summer Schools Programme for Disadvantaged Pupils: Key Findings for Schools Research Report*. London: DfE.

Department for Education (2014a). *Assessment Principles*. London: DfE.

Department for Education (2014b). *National Curriculum and Assessment from September 2014: Information for Schools*. London: DfE.

Department for Education (2014c). *Statutory Policies for Schools Advice on the Policies and Documents That Governing Bodies and Proprietors of Schools Are Required to Have by Law*. London: DfE.

Department for Education (2014d). *National Curriculum in England: English Programmes of Study*. London: DfE.

Department for Education (2016a). *Progress 8 Measure in 2016, 2017, and 2018 Guide for Maintained Secondary Schools, Academies and Free Schools.* London: DfE.

Department for Education (2016b). *Essential School Maintenance: A Guide for Schools.* London: DfE.

Department for Education (2016c). *Eliminating Unnecessary Workload Associated with Data Management.* London: DfE.

Department for Education (2018a). *Careers Guidance and Access for Education and Training Providers: Statutory Guidance for Governing Bodies, School Leaders and School Staff.* London: DfE.

Department for Education (2018b). *Induction for Newly Qualified Teachers (England): Statutory Guidance for Appropriate Bodies, Headteachers, School Staff and Governing Bodies.* London: DfE.

Department for Education (2019a). *Analysis of OfSTED Good and Outstanding Schools.* London: DfE.

Department for Education (2019b). *School Teachers' Pay and Conditions Document 2019 and Guidance on Schoolteachers' Pay and Conditions.* London: DfE.

Department for Education (2019c). *Teacher Workload Survey 2019.* London: DfE.

Department for Education (2019d). *Teacher Recruitment and Retention Strategy.* London: DfE.

Department for Education (2019e). *Teacher Appraisal and Capability A Model Policy for Schools.* London: DfE.

Department for Education (2020a). *Academies Financial Handbook 2020.* London: DfE.

Department for Education (2020b). *Checklist for School Leaders to Support Full Opening: Behaviour and Attendance.* London: DfE.

Department for Education (2020c). *School Census 2020 to 2021 Business and Technical Specification, Version 1.5.* London: DfE.

Department for Education (2021). Find and Compare Schools in England. www.compar e-school-performance.service.gov.uk/schools-bytype?step=default&table=schools &region=all-england&for=ofsted. Accessed 9.1.2021.

Dunford, J. (2016). *The School Leadership Journey.* Woodbridge: John Catt.

Education Endowment Foundation (2018). *Teaching and Learning Toolkit.* London: EEF.

Elkin, S. (2007). *100 Ideas for Secondary School Assemblies.* London: Continuum.

European Commission (2018). *Quality Assurance for School Development: Guiding Principles for Policy Development on Quality Assurance in School Education.* Brussels: European Commission.

Foster, J. (2018). *Jumpstart! Assemblies: Ideas and Activities for Assemblies in Primary Schools.* London: Routledge.

Gawande, A. (2011). *The Checklist Manifesto: How to Get Things Right.* London: Profile Books.

Gershon, M. (2009). *How to Use Assessment for Learning in the Classroom: A Complete Guide.* Scotts Valley, CA, USA: CreateSpace Independent Publishing Platform.

Gill, T. (2017). *The Impact of the Introduction of Progress 8 on the Uptake and Provision of Qualifications in English Schools.* Cambridge: Cambridge University.

Gillard, D. (2018). Education in England: A history. Article to be found at: www.educat ionengland.org.uk/history/timeline.html. Accessed 29.10.20.

Hall, J. (2020). 25 Tips to Create a Master Calendar That Works. www.calendar.com/blog/ create-a-master-calendar/. Accessed 19.11.2020.

Hanson, T.E., Austin, G., and Lee-Bayha, J. (2004). *Ensuring That No Child is Left Behind: How Are Pupil Health Risks & Resilience Related to the Academic Progress of Schools?* San Francisco, CA: WestEd.

Harpham, M. (2020). *Progress Plain and Simple: What Every Teacher Needs to Know About Improving Pupil Progress.* London: Routledge.

Heller, R. and Hindle, T. (1998). *Essential Managers Manual.* London: Dorking Kindersley.

Higton, J., Leonardi, S., Richards, N. and Choudhoury, A. (2017). *Teacher Workload Survey 2016*. London: DfE.

Higton, J., Leonardi, S., Richards, N., Choudoury, A., Sofroniou, N., and Owen, D. (2017). *Teacher Workload Survey, 2016*. London: Department for Education.

Jerrim, J. and Sims, S. (2019). *The Teaching and Learning International Survey (TALIS) 2018*. London: UCL.

Joint Council for Qualifications (2020). *A Guide to the Awarding Bodies Appeals Processes*. London: JCQ.

Kelly, A. and Downey, C. (2011). *Using Effectiveness Data for School Improvement: Developing and utilising Metrics*. London: Routledge.

Kyriakides, L. and Creemers, B. (2008). A longitudinal study on the stability over time of school and teacher effects on pupil outcomes, in *Oxford Review of Education*, 34(5), 521–545.

Law, S. and Glover, D. (2000). *Educational Leadership and Learning: Practice, Policy, and Research*. Milton Keynes: OUP.

Lenon, B. (2017). *Much Promise: Successful Schools in England*. Woodbridge: John Catt.

McCluskey, G. (2017). Mapping, measuring, and monitoring achievement: Can a new evaluation framework help schools challenge inequalities? in *Improving Schools*, 20(1), 5–17.

Muijs, D., Kyriakides, L., van der Werf, G., Creemers, B., Timperley, H., and Earl, L. (2014). State of the Art – Teacher effectiveness and professional learning, in *School Effectiveness and School Improvement*, 25(2), 231–256.

Nasen (2014). *Tracking Progress and Managing Provision*. Tamworth, Staffordshire: Nasen.

NFER (2013). *Top Tips for Running a Successful Summer School*. London: NFER.

Offenberg, R.M. (2004). Inferring adequate yearly progress of schools from pupil achievement in highly mobile communities, in *Journal of Education for Pupils Placed at Risk*, 9(4), 337–355.

Ofsted (2003). *Good Assessment in Secondary Schools*. London: Ofsted.

Ofsted (2017). *Reception Curriculum in Good and Outstanding Primary Schools: Bold Beginnings*. London: Ofsted.

Ofsted (2019a). *Educational Inspection Framework: Overview of the Research*. London: Ofsted.

Ofsted (2019b). *The School Inspection Handbook*. London: Ofsted.

Ofsted (2019c). *Teacher Well-Being at Work in Schools and Further Education Providers*. London: Ofsted.

Ofsted (2019d). *Analysis of Ofsted Good and Outstanding Schools*. London: Ofsted.

Paterson, C. (2013). *Measuring What Matters: Secondary School Accountability Indicators That Benefit All*. London: Centre Forum and Pearson.

Percival, A. and Tranter, S. (2006). *How to Run Your School Successfully*. London: Continuum.

PSHE Association (2017). *PSHE Education – Programme of Study Key Stages 1–5*. London: PSHE Association.

Reynolds, D., Sammons, S., De Fraine, B., Van Damme, J., Townsend, T., Teddlie, C., and Stringfield, S. (2014). Educational effectiveness research (EER): A state-of-the-art review, in *School Effectiveness and School Improvement*, 25(2), 197–230.

Salvato, N. (2019). *How to Win Your School Appeal: An Easy to Follow Up-to-Date Guide to School Admission Appeals*. Salvato on Kindle, Kindle Digital version, available from Amazon.com (ASIN: B07Z5G1LGX).

Sedgwick, F. (2006). *100 Ideas for Primary School Assemblies*. London: Continuum.

Slater, H., Davies, N, and Burgess, S. (2009). *Do Teachers Matter? Measuring the Variation in Teacher Effectiveness in England*. London: Centre for Market and Public Organisation.

Solomon, Y. and Lewin, C. (2016). Measuring "progress": Performativity as both driver and constraint in school innovation, in *Journal of Education Policy*, 31(2), 226–238.

Sutton Trust (2015). *Developing Teachers: Improving Professional Development for Teachers*. London: Sutton Trust.

Tomlinson, J. (2020). *School Appeals Explained: A Clear Guide for Parents and Carers to Help Them Understand How School Appeals Work and How to Prepare for their School Appeal*. Kindle Digital version, available from Amazon.com (ASIN: B00X5UB5PG.

UKCES (2014). *The Future of Work Jobs and Skills in 2030*. London: UKCES.

Wiliam, D. (2011). *Teacher Quality: What It Is, Why It Matters and How to Get More of It*. London: Institute of Education.

Wiliam, D. (2018). *Embedded Formative Assessment* (Second edition). Bloomington, IN: Solution Tree Press.

Index

Printed in Great Britain
by Amazon

33827836R00134